Unlocking the Why: The New Science of Motivating Anyone, Anywhere

By Meagan Hopper

Introduction: The Leader I Never Had

I had been dreaming of working for this company since I was three years old. It wasn't just a career goal; it was a core part of my identity.

So I did what anyone does when their lifelong dream comes true: I bet everything on it. I flew across the country to meet my car, my cat tucked in a carrier under the seat in front of me for her very first flight. I left behind my family, my friends, and every ounce of familiarity I had ever known. I was running on pure adrenaline and the certainty that I had finally, truly made it.

Then, reality hit.

In my first year, I went through five different bosses. I felt like a ghost floating through the hallways of my own dream, doing tasks without context, belonging to no one, completely directionless. The final blow came in the form of a manager who crystallized everything that was wrong. During a check-in, after I mentioned having lunch with some colleagues, he looked at me coolly.

"You shouldn't be friends with people you work with," he said.

There was no effort to understand my perspective, no interest in what was important to me or what I needed to succeed. Looking back, I see it with perfect clarity: He was a boss, not a leader. A boss directs tasks and tries to shut down your human side to make you a more efficient cog in the machine. A leader knows your human side is the very source of your greatest potential.

A Symptom of a Broken System

What I didn't realize then was that my experience wasn't just a stroke of bad luck with a single bad boss. It was a symptom of an outdated, industrial-era management operating system—an operating system that is currently causing a crisis in the modern workplace.

We are standing at a critical intersection. On one side, we are facing the "Silver Tsunami"—a massive wave of veteran experts retiring and walking out the door. Because the old management playbook failed to tap into their fundamental human drives, they are leaving without transferring their decades of irreplaceable institutional knowledge to the next generation.

On the other side, a new workforce is arriving. These incoming generations completely reject the old "shut up and do your job" mentality. They demand purpose. They expect transparency. Above all, they require authentic communication. The old top-down directives are failing spectacularly.

To bridge this massive gap, we have to fundamentally change how we lead. We have to stop managing tasks and start unearthing what truly motivates the humans doing those tasks.

The Promise of This Book

Years later, in a new role in a new location, I became a leader myself. And in that moment, I made a decision. I would step in to be the leader I never had.

That decision changed everything. It became the foundation of my leadership philosophy, a philosophy built not on theory, but on the scar tissue of my own experience.

While the framework in this book will very likely maximize your team's quarterly outputs, this is not a manual simply about squeezing more productivity out of a broken system. It's a manual about unleashing human potential. Inside, you will find a clear, actionable framework to move beyond the transactional and build something transformational. We will cover how to:

- **Discover Your Own Leadership Why:** To become the leader your team needs, you first have to understand the purpose that drives you.
- **Unearth Your Employees' Why:** You will learn how to shift from listening to reply, to truly listening to understand, getting to the heart of what motivates each person on your team.

- **Adapt Your Leadership to Their Why:** You will learn to connect their purpose to their daily work, turning their job into a calling and unlocking a level of performance and commitment you've only dreamed of.

The revolving door of talent doesn't have to be your reality. This book was written for every leader who refuses to let their people feel as lost, invisible, and disconnected as I once did.

It's time to stop being a boss and start being the leader your team is waiting for. Let's get started.

Chapter 1: Beyond the "What": From Organizational Why to Individual Why

You've probably been in a room like this before.

It's the annual all-hands meeting. The lights are dimmed, a slick presentation is on the screen, and the CEO is on stage, delivering a passionate speech about the company's mission.

"We're not just selling software," they declare, "we are empowering small businesses to change the world!" or "We don't just make products; we build communities!"

There's a swell of applause. People feel a genuine surge of inspiration.

For the rest of the week, that energy lingers. You see the new catchphrase in email signatures, you hear it repeated in team meetings, and the official highlights video gets shared around.

But then, the slow fade begins. The initial glow of the big mission gets worn down by the relentless reality of the day-to-day.

The engineer has a looming deadline. The salesperson has a tough quota to hit. The HR manager is dealing with a complex payroll issue. The lofty, world-changing mission feels very, very far away from the blinking cursor on their screen.

This is the fundamental disconnect in the modern workplace. And it's not because our company missions are bad. On the contrary, thanks to the groundbreaking work of thinkers like Simon Sinek, leaders have become incredibly good at defining their organization's purpose.

His concept of the "Golden Circle" taught us to "Start With Why"—to articulate *why* our company exists beyond the 'what' we do or the 'how' we do it.

This **Organizational Why** is essential. It's the company's North Star. It guides strategy, inspires marketing, and gives the entire organization a direction to move in. It's the destination on the map.

But here is the truth that so many leaders miss: *A map is useless if the runners are too exhausted to run.*

The Connection Gap

While the organization has a "Why," each person who works there has one, too.

This **Individual Why** is their own personal, internal drive. It's the unique combination of passions, skills, and desired impacts that gives them a sense of fulfillment. It's the reason they get out of bed in the morning, beyond the need for a paycheck.

Psychologists Edward Deci and Richard Ryan formalized this in their *Self-Determination Theory,* which argues that human beings have three innate psychological needs: **Competence** (feeling effective), **Autonomy** (feeling in control), and **Relatedness** (feeling connected).

When a job feels disconnected from an individual's core drives, it starves these needs.

The problem is, we rarely make the effort to understand this second, more personal "Why." We show our employees the map (the company's mission) and simply expect them to start *running*, assuming their inspiration will come from the destination alone.

For most people, it doesn't work. The gap between the CEO's grand vision and their daily tasks is just too wide.

We can call this the **Connection Gap**. It's the space between "We are changing the world!" and "I have to finish these 37 spreadsheet tabs by Friday."

The Anatomy of the Disconnect

When that gap feels too large for too long, people disengage. They slow to a walk. They "quiet quit."

"Quiet quitting" isn't usually a loud rebellion; it's a silent withdrawal. It's the employee whose camera is always mysteriously off during virtual meetings. It's the star performer who suddenly stops offering new ideas, delivering only the minimum viable effort required to not get fired. It's the physical and mental exhaustion that comes from running the marathon without any internal motivation to sustain the pace. When the daily tasks feel entirely disconnected from any personal sense of purpose, the psychological toll is profound.

But this Connection Gap isn't just an individual retention issue; it is a systemic business crisis, compounded by massive demographic shifts in the modern workplace.

Consider the "Silver Tsunami." The largest generations in the workforce are actively retiring, taking decades of institutional, hard-earned knowledge with them out the door. Traditional management completely fails to incentivize these veterans to transfer their wisdom before they leave. If leaders do not understand an employee's Individual Why—if we fail to tap into their natural drive to mentor or leave a legacy—that irreplaceable knowledge is gone forever.

At the exact same time, we are facing the new rules of engagement brought by the incoming workforce. Millennials and Gen Z are not willing to accept the old "pay your dues" or "because I said so" mentalities of the past. They demand transparency, purpose, and authentic connection in their daily work. They don't just prefer a different management style; they require a completely different language.

This means leaders must fundamentally change how they communicate. The old, top-down directives no longer work. Modern leadership requires moving away from the defensive habit of *listening to reply*—simply waiting for your turn to speak or issue a command—and shifting entirely toward *listening to understand.*

Authentic communication is the only bridge across this generational divide. If you cannot connect with what truly drives your people, you will lose the knowledge of the past and fail to engage the talent of the future. Eventually, these disconnected employees will leave in search of a race where the running itself feels like it *matters*—to them.

A Story from the Wild: The Offer That Missed the Point

The cost of this disconnect is profound, and it happens at every level of an organization. I've experienced it firsthand.

A few years ago, I was on a trip to South Dakota with my parents to celebrate my father's retirement. We were staying at a beautiful farmhouse bed-and-breakfast, horses and all.

The night before we were checking out, the owner approached me to confirm a suspicion he had. After a firm handshake, he smiled and said, "You must be in the industry, too."

He told me about the company his whole family worked for—one of the biggest construction companies in the US, actually—and mentioned they were trying to increase diversity by bringing in more capable women.

Funny enough, the night before, I had been lamenting to my parents that I was feeling unfulfilled in my current role, so I said I'd be interested in talking.

The interview process was exciting. Everyone remarked on my ability to communicate, but one senior leader, in particular, lit up when he learned about my background in alternative health and wellness.

"That's so different," he said. "What else could you bring to our company?"

We talked about creating new training offerings and improving the employee experience. For the first time in a while, I felt seen for my unique potential, not just my resume.

But when the official offer came, it was for a standard role, completely disconnected from the exciting, purpose-driven possibilities we had discussed.

The company saw a 'what'—a role to fill. I had seen a 'why'—a chance to make a unique impact.

In that moment of disappointment, I realized that one of my biggest personal drivers is to make the journey easier for those who want to move forward but don't know how. The offer failed because it spoke to a job description, not to my Individual Why.

The Map and the Marathon

Think of your team's work as a marathon:

- The **Organizational Why** is the **finish line** on the map. It's the shared goal that everyone is running towards. As a leader, you must constantly point to it.
- The **Individual Why** is the **runner's heart and stamina**. It's their personal, internal drive that keeps their legs moving when the course gets steep and their energy is low.

A great team of runners needs both a clear map and the deep, personal motivation to keep going. A leader who only talks about the finish line but ignores the exhaustion and motivation of their runners will find their team collapsing midway through the race.

The art of modern leadership is to be the bridge between the two. Your job is to be the **Head Coach** who runs alongside them, understands what fuels each person's internal drive, and then shows them how their personal effort helps the entire team advance toward that shared, meaningful finish line.

So, what exactly is this "Individual Why?" It's not some vague, mystical feeling. It's a tangible concept that usually sits at the intersection of three things:

- **Their Passions:** What topics, problems, or activities give them energy?
- **Their Skills:** What are their unique, innate strengths?
- **Their Desired Impact:** What outcome makes them feel a deep sense of satisfaction?

When you, as a leader, understand this unique combination for each person on your team, you hold the key. You can stop trying to motivate with broad, corporate mission statements and start connecting with the powerful, personal purpose that already exists within them.

A Deeper Look: Common Questions

As you begin this journey, a few common questions might arise. Let's address them head-on.

"But what if our company's mission *is* really inspiring?" That's fantastic. A strong Organizational Why is a huge advantage. But it's not a substitute for understanding the individual.

Think of a championship football team. Every single player, from the star quarterback to the offensive lineman, shares the same goal: win the

Super Bowl. That's their Organizational Why. But the quarterback's Individual Why might be the thrill of executing a perfect, game-winning pass. The lineman's Individual Why might be the satisfaction of physically protecting his teammates and dominating his opponent.

Same goal, completely different drivers. A great coach understands and speaks to both.

"What if my employee says they're just here for a paycheck?" Many leaders hear this and stop digging. They take it at face value. But more often than not, "I'm just here for the paycheck" is a defense mechanism.

It's what people say after they've given up hope of finding real meaning in their work. It's a symptom of past bad management, not a permanent state of being.

The methods in this book are designed to re-awaken that dormant desire for purpose. When you show a genuine interest in what truly drives them, you give them permission to want more from their work than just a salary.

In the next chapter, we'll start this journey by looking inward. Before you can become the Head Coach for your team, you first have to understand what keeps you in the race.

It's time to discover your own leadership "Why."

Chapter 2: First, Lead Yourself: Discovering Your Own Leadership Why

The calendar alarm chimes. Your 10 a.m. meeting is starting, which means you have exactly one hour before your 11 a.m. budget review, which is immediately followed by a project sync and then a 1-on-1. You spend the day jumping between video calls, answering urgent emails, and putting out small fires.

At 6 p.m., you finally shut your laptop, feeling a familiar wave of exhaustion. You were busy all day, but what did you actually build? What impact did you really have?

For many managers, this is the daily reality. We get so caught up in the relentless activity of management that we lose touch with the profound purpose of leadership. We become professional administrators, meeting-schedulers, and problem-solvers. In the process, the spark that once drew us to leadership begins to fade.

Before you can become the Head Coach for your team, you first have to understand what keeps you in the race. You must get clear on your own motivation, your own purpose, and your own definition of a job well done.

It's the first rule of emergency response for a reason: you have to put on your own oxygen mask first. You cannot guide a team toward purpose and fulfillment if you are running on the fumes of obligation. You cannot have authentic conversations about what drives your people if you are disconnected from what drives you.

Your team will sense the disconnect immediately. They will see a manager going through the motions, and they will respond in kind. To become the leader your team is waiting for, you must first become the leader you are meant to be. This starts by discovering your own Leadership Why.

The Dangers of a "Why-less" Leader

When a leader loses touch with their "Why," they often don't notice it at first. The change is buried under an avalanche of monotonous activity. The days fill with administrative tasks, back-to-back meetings, and endless small fires, leaving little time or energy for genuine leadership.

The Disappearance of Margin In this state of perpetual, reactive motion, the first things to disappear are your essential human margins. You stop budgeting time to decompress between meetings. You eat lunch staring at your screen, taking shallow, bite-sized breaths while you type, tricking yourself into believing that sacrificing your breaks makes you more productive.

In reality, failing to simply breathe and be in your body depletes the cognitive and emotional reserves required to truly show up for your team. You cannot listen to understand if your nervous system is utterly exhausted. Without that baseline of physiological and mental well-being, genuine relationship-building becomes impossible. You stop seeing your team as people to connect with and start seeing them as interruptions to your workflow. The interactions become purely transactional.

It's in this state of reactive busyness that a leader's perspective begins to drift.

A Story from the Wild: The Manager's Drift
Consider Mark, a brilliant software engineer promoted to manager. As an engineer, his "Why" was clear: solving complex problems and building elegant code. But as a manager, his calendar was instantly filled with budget reviews and HR paperwork.

Overwhelmed, he started focusing on what he thought his director wanted: clean status reports and hitting deadlines at all costs. His 1-on-1s with his team devolved from collaborative brainstorming sessions into rapid-fire status checks: "Is it done yet?"

Six months in, his best engineer—someone who reminded him of his younger self—was visibly disengaged. Mark was succeeding at the tasks of management but failing at the purpose of leadership, and he felt more exhausted than ever.

Lacking the internal compass of their own "Why," a leader like Mark starts looking for external validation. Their primary focus shifts from the people they lead to the people who lead them. This is where the line between a true leader and a boss becomes clear. A leader remains accountable to their team. A boss becomes preoccupied with the perceptions of their higher-ups.

This shift in focus—whether driven by fear, corporate pressure, or simply the exhaustion of the daily grind—is what leads to predictable behaviors:

- They become transactional.
- They focus only on metrics.
- Their feedback becomes hollow.
- They micromanage.

A leader without a "Why" is the very definition of the "boss" I described in my own story—the kind who creates an environment of anxiety and obligation, not one of purpose and trust.

The Holistic Cost: Why Your Life and Leadership are Connected Here is the secret that traditional business books rarely tell you: the exhaustion of a "Why-less" leader does not magically disappear when you pull into your driveway at night.

We like to pretend that work and life are two separate buckets, but you are one whole person. When you spend eight to ten hours a day starved of intrinsic motivation, operating out of alignment with your core drivers, that depletion bleeds into every other area of your life.

It shows up as having zero patience with your family after a long day. It shows up as ordering takeout again because you don't have the mental bandwidth to cook. It shows up as abandoning the hobbies and health routines that used to give you energy, simply because you have nothing left in the tank.

Your leadership health and your personal wellness are inextricably linked. You cannot be a burned-out, deeply unfulfilled human being at 5:59 p.m. and expect to be a vibrant, empathetic, purpose-driven leader at 9:00 a.m. the next morning.

This is exactly why, before I dive into team dynamics with my clients, I often take them through a comprehensive Life & Leadership Audit. We have to zoom out and look at the whole picture. We evaluate where their energy is actually going, how their daily habits support or sabotage their professional goals, and where the misalignments are draining their vitality.

When leaders engage in coaching, we don't just fix their 1-on-1 agendas; we reconstruct their foundation. We align their career ambitions with their holistic well-being, because a leader who is healthy, grounded, and clear on their personal purpose is a force of nature in the boardroom.

So, let's make sure that's not you. The following exercise is designed to cut through the daily noise and reconnect you with your core purpose as a leader.

Your Self-Discovery Exercise: A Quick Guide

Grab a notebook or open a new document. As you approach the following three questions, keep these two principles in mind to get the most out of your reflection.

First, hunt for a powerful memory, not just a "happy" one. This reminds me of a lesson from Harry Potter and the Prisoner of Azkaban. When Professor Lupin is teaching Harry to produce a Patronus Charm, he tells him he must focus on a single, very happy memory. Harry struggles until he lands on the memory of seeing his parents in the Mirror of Erised. As he notes, it wasn't a happy memory, not really, as it was tinged with loss. But it was powerful. It was the most powerful feeling he knew, and it was the one that worked.

That's what you are looking for in your "Peak Moment"—a memory of deep fulfillment and impact. The size of the moment doesn't matter, but the power of the feeling does.

Second, be brutally honest, even if your answers feel "selfish." This exercise is about uncovering your fundamental drivers, not writing a perfect, altruistic mission statement. If your gut answer to the "Legacy" question is, "I want them to say I was the smartest leader they ever had," don't judge it— write it down. That's valuable data. You can then reframe it into a purpose: "My purpose is to use my expertise to solve our team's most complex problems." Be honest about the raw driver first, then you can refine it into a purpose that serves others.

Question 1: The Peak Moment Think back over your career as a leader. Picture that specific time—a day, a week, a project—where you felt completely energized and alive. A time you went home feeling a deep sense of satisfaction, thinking, "This is why I do this."

- What were you doing?
- Who were you with?
- What was the specific challenge or situation?
- What was the outcome that made you so proud?

Question 2: The Unique Contribution Forget your job title and official responsibilities for a moment. What is the unique impact that you, as a person, bring to your team? What do people consistently come to you for, beyond your formal authority?

Question 3: The Legacy Imagine it's five years from now. You run into a former member of your team in an airport. After you greet each other, they turn to the person they are with and say, "This was my leader when I was at [Company]. They were the one who..." How do you want them to finish that sentence?

Putting It All Together: Your Leadership Why Statement

Now, let's synthesize your answers into a simple, powerful statement. This isn't a corporate mission statement; it's a personal declaration.

Use the following template as a starting point, filling in the blanks with words and ideas from your reflections above.

My purpose as a leader is to [ACTION FROM QUESTION 2] so that my team feels [FEELING FROM QUESTION 1] in order to [LEGACY FROM QUESTION 3].

For example: "My purpose as a leader is to create psychological safety and find common ground so that my team feels harmonious and collaborative in order to build a place where they can trust each other and do their best work."

Take a few minutes and write your own.

This statement is now your compass. When you're feeling lost in the weeds of management, it will remind you of your purpose. When you have to make a difficult decision, it will guide you. It is the foundation of authentic leadership.

Now that you've put on your own oxygen mask and can breathe clearly, it's time to help the people on your team. It's time to learn the art of discovering their Why.

Part 2: The Art of Discovery

Chapter 3: The Archeologist's Toolkit: How to Uncover Your Employee's Why

Think of yourself as an archeologist. An archeologist doesn't show up to a dig site with a stick of dynamite. They don't just blast through the surface to get to the treasure. They arrive with a set of specialized tools—brushes, trowels, and sifters. They are patient. They work with care, gently clearing away the dust and debris layer by layer, knowing that the context and the story are just as valuable as the artifact itself.

Remember the scene in *Indiana Jones and the Last Crusade* where Indy is in the Venice library, meticulously sweeping away centuries of dust and grime to reveal the Roman numeral "X" on the floor? It's that slow, careful process of revelation—not brute force—that uncovers the true path forward.

This is the mindset you must adopt when seeking to understand your employee's "Why". You are not a mechanic looking to fix a problem or a doctor trying to make a diagnosis. You are an archeologist of human potential, looking to uncover the valuable, hidden drivers that give a person their energy and purpose. Your job is not to judge what you find, but to understand it with respect and curiosity.

Before we open the toolkit, let's establish the crucial principles for any successful dig.

Setting the Stage: The Prerequisite of Psychological Safety

Before you ask a single question, you have to prepare the environment. If you walk into a 1-on-1 meeting radiating stress, rushing through your agenda, and treating the conversation like a checklist, your employee's nervous system will immediately go on the defensive. You cannot excavate a person's deepest professional drivers if they do not feel safe enough to expose them.

Creating psychological safety starts with regulating your own energy. If you are feeling anxious or rushed, take a moment before the meeting to center yourself. Simply breathe. Take a deep, intentional breath and consciously be in your body, rather than trapped in your racing thoughts. Grounding yourself signals to the other person that you are fully present. It shows them that for the next thirty minutes, they are your only priority.

A Crucial Note: The Whole Person

Your archeological site is not limited to the hours of 9-to-5. Your employees are whole people, and their "Why" doesn't turn on and off when they clock in and out.

The person who spends their weekends meticulously building furniture in their garage doesn't magically lose their passion for creating things on Monday morning. The employee who coaches their daughter's soccer team doesn't leave their love of mentoring at the field. Paying attention to these clues is not prying; it's a profound act of seeing someone for who they truly are.

A Clue in the Frustration: Listen for What Drains Them

While stories about high points are fantastic, you can often get an even clearer signal of someone's "Why" by paying attention to what *drains* them. People's frustrations are an unintentional roadmap to their core drivers.

Pay attention to their complaints, their sighs, and the tasks they procrastinate on. The energy sink is just as telling as the energy source.

With this mindset in place, you are ready to open the toolkit.

Tool #1: "High-Point" Storytelling

The easiest and most natural place to start your excavation is with a story. A person's energy naturally shifts when they talk about experiences that were genuinely fulfilling. Your job is to create the space for that story and then observe what unfolds.

How to Use It: In your next 1-on-1, try opening with one of these prompts:

- "Tell me about a time at work—either here or in a past job—where you felt completely in your element. A time you were totally energized and maybe even lost track of time".
- "Thinking back on the last year, what was a project or a moment that you felt the most proud of? What was it that made you feel that way?".

Reading the Unspoken Language: As they tell their story, listen with your ears *and* your eyes. Words can be rehearsed, but physiology rarely lies. You are looking for a shift in their baseline behavior.

- **Watch their posture:** Do they suddenly sit up straighter or lean forward across the desk?
- **Listen to their pacing:** Does their speech speed up? Do they start talking with their hands when they are normally quite still?
- **Notice their vocal tone:** Does their voice get louder or more animated?

These physical signs are direct pointers to their "Why". When you see that physical shift, pay close attention to the core theme they are discussing. Was it the collaboration, the problem-solving, the mentoring, the creating, or the organizing that lit them up?

A Story from the Wild: The Quiet Coder's Surprise A manager named Sarah was struggling with a software developer, 'Ben'. Ben was technically brilliant but incredibly quiet and seemed disengaged in team meetings. He did his work and went home. In their next 1-on-1, Sarah decided to try this tool. She asked him, "Ben, tell me about a project where you felt the most energized".

Sarah expected him to talk about a complex piece of code he'd written. Instead, Ben's face lit up for the first time she could remember. He said, "Last summer, when we had that intern, Laura. I got to show her how our system works. At the end of the summer, she gave a presentation and she was just... so good. I felt so proud".

In that single, two-minute story, Sarah's entire perception of Ben shifted. She thought he was a classic solo-performer, but she had just discovered a powerful, hidden "Teacher" archetype. She had been giving him the wrong kind of work and the wrong kind of recognition for over a year.

Tool #2: Career Journey Mapping

This tool helps you see patterns over time. An employee's career path may seem random, but it almost always contains a consistent thread of what motivates and demotivates them.

How to Use It: Ask your employee to sketch out their career journey on a whiteboard or a piece of paper, plotting the key roles or projects on a timeline. Then, have them map the "highs" and "lows"—the peaks of fulfillment and the valleys of frustration.

Once the map is drawn, you can explore it together with questions like:

- "Looking at these high points, what do they all have in common?".
- "What were the consistent themes or conditions during the low points?".

Tool #3: The "5 Whys" for Motivation

This technique, inspired by a child's relentless curiosity, is about gently pushing past surface-level answers to uncover the core driver.

How to Use It: Start with an observation, and then gently ask "Why?" (or a softer variation like "What was it about that that mattered to you?") up to five times to dig deeper. Your tone is crucial; it should be one of genuine curiosity, not interrogation.

A Deeper Look: Navigating the Conversation

As you start using these tools, you might run into a few common conversational roadblocks. Here's how to navigate them.

Challenge: Navigating the Silence When you ask someone a profound question about their fulfillment, they rarely have an immediate, polished answer ready to go. Often, there will be silence. For many leaders, a quiet pause stretching past three seconds feels agonizing. The instinct is to jump in, rephrase the question, or answer it for them to ease the tension.

Don't. The magic of these conversations often happens in the pregnant pause. Think of the interaction as fluid and unscripted. You must stay present in the moment and react to what they actually give you, rather than sticking rigidly to your planned list of questions. Let the scene breathe. When you allow the silence to stretch, you give them the cognitive space to actually search their memory and find an authentic answer.

Challenge: The "I Don't Know" Employee You ask for a high point, and they just shrug and say, "I don't know, nothing really stands out". This isn't a dead end; it's a sign that you need to lower the stakes.

The question may feel too big. Try breaking the question down into a more bite-sized, recent scope:

- "Okay, how about just last week? Was there any 30-minute period where you felt like you were in a state of flow?".
- "What was the best part of your day yesterday?".

Sometimes, the most powerful clues are found in the smallest moments. An answer like, "I guess when I finally got my inbox organized," is a huge clue for a potential Stabilizer.

Challenge: The Fear of Being "Nosy" Many leaders feel a natural hesitation to ask questions that seem too personal. It can feel like you're prying. The key to overcoming this is *transparency*.

Frame the conversation by stating your positive intent upfront. You can say: *"I'm asking these questions because my goal is to make sure I'm aligning the work you do with the things you actually find energizing and fulfilling. The better I understand what drives you, the better I can support you"*.

This isn't about digging into their private life. It's about understanding their professional energy. When your intent is clearly to help, not to judge, people will almost always open up.

Challenge: The Risk of Misinterpreting the Clues After hearing Ben's story about the intern, Sarah's first thought was, "Great, Ben's a Teacher!". But it's important not to jump to a permanent conclusion based on one story.

Treat your findings as a hypothesis, not a verdict. The next step is to test the hypothesis. Sarah could give Ben a small, low-risk "Teacher" task, like asking him to lead a 15-minute demo on a new tool for the team. If he lights up and does a fantastic job, it's strong confirmation. If he seems burdened by it, her hypothesis might be wrong, and that's okay too. The goal is to be a curious detective, not a judge who delivers a final verdict.

Chapter 4: The Science of Being Seen: Why Empathy is an Economic Imperative

In the design and construction industry, safety on a job site is paramount. You wear a high-visibility vest or a brightly colored hard hat so you stand out against the background of heavy machinery and raw materials. The goal is simple and transactional: make sure the people around you know you are there so you don't get hurt.

But there is a massive, fundamental difference between being visible and being *seen*.

Visibility is a baseline requirement. It means your name is on the org chart, your face is in the Zoom square, and your output is measured on a spreadsheet. Most management operating systems are built entirely around visibility.

Being *seen*, however, is about profound connection. It means a leader understands the human being behind the hard hat or the laptop screen. It means they recognize your unique drivers, your fears, and your innate potential. This distinction is so critical to modern leadership that it became the foundation of my consultancy, HiVis Hoodie LLC, and our core motto: *"Don't Just Be Visible. Be Seen."*

When an employee is merely visible, they give you their compliance. When an employee is truly seen, they give you their commitment.

If that sounds like a soft, philosophical sentiment, it isn't. It is a biological reality backed by deep neurological research. The act of truly seeing the people behind the work is the single greatest driver of high performance, innovation, and retention in the modern workplace. Let's look at the science.

The Neurochemistry of Leadership and "Survival Mode"

Every interaction you have with an employee triggers a measurable neurochemical and physiological response. To understand the impact of leadership on performance, we have to understand how the brain processes its environment.

As researcher, author, and neuroscientist Dr. Joe Dispenza has extensively documented, when human beings operate in a state of stress, fear, or disconnection, we are fundamentally living in "survival mode." When a leader acts as a traditional "boss"—managing through intimidation, micromanagement, or transactional demands—they trigger the employee's sympathetic nervous system.

Dr. Dispenza's research illustrates that in this survival state, the brain shifts into erratic, high-beta brainwaves. The body is flooded with stress hormones like cortisol and adrenaline. The brain perceives the lack of psychological safety as a literal, physical threat.

In this state of "fight or flight," the brain aggressively reroutes energy away from the prefrontal cortex—the area responsible for complex problem-solving, creativity, and collaboration. As Dispenza notes, when you are in survival mode, your focus narrows entirely to the external threat. An employee flooded with cortisol cannot innovate; they can only survive. They will keep their head down, do exactly what they are told, and avoid taking any risks.

But Dr. Dispenza's findings also reveal the incredible power of the opposite state: coherence.

When an employee is truly *seen*—when a leader takes the time to uncover their "Why" and actively listens to understand—the brain's response completely changes. The perceived threat disappears. The body moves out of the sympathetic nervous system and activates the parasympathetic nervous system (rest and digest).

The heart and brain synchronize. This state of coherence allows the brain to move into alpha and theta brainwave states, and the body releases a cocktail of positive neurochemicals, including oxytocin (the chemical of trust and bonding) and dopamine (the chemical of reward and motivation).

This chemical shift literally unlocks the executive functioning of the brain. The employee is now biologically primed to learn, adapt, solve complex problems, and push the boundaries of their potential. By making your employee feel *seen*, you are not just being kind; you are chemically optimizing their brain for high performance.

The Data: Google's Project Aristotle

If the neurochemistry proves the concept at the individual level, Google proved it at the organizational level.

In 2012, Google launched "Project Aristotle," a massive, multi-year study to find the perfect algorithm for building a highly productive team. They analyzed hundreds of teams across the company, looking for the magic combination of traits. Did the best teams have the highest aggregate IQs? Did they share similar educational backgrounds? Did they hang out together outside of work?

The data researchers were stunned by the results. The "who" part of the equation didn't matter nearly as much as the "how." The researchers found that the single most important metric for a team's success was **psychological safety**.

Psychological safety is the shared belief that a team is safe for interpersonal risk-taking. It is the environment created when a leader proves that an employee will not be punished, humiliated, or marginalized for speaking up with ideas, questions, concerns, or mistakes.

You cannot manufacture psychological safety with a ping-pong table in the breakroom or a catchy corporate value statement. Psychological safety is built one 1-on-1 at a time. It is established when a leader sits across from an employee, uses their Archeologist's Toolkit, and proves that they care about the employee's Individual Why.

The ROI of Empathy

For decades, empathy was dismissed in corporate environments as a "soft skill"—a nice-to-have trait for HR professionals, but completely unnecessary for serious business leaders driving bottom-line results.

The data now proves that this outdated mindset is a massive financial liability.

A comprehensive study by Catalyst, a global nonprofit researching workplace inclusion, surveyed nearly 900 employees across various industries to measure the direct effects of empathetic leadership. The findings were staggering:

- **Innovation:** 61% of employees with highly empathetic senior leaders reported being innovative at work, compared to only 13% of employees with less empathetic leaders.
- **Engagement:** 76% of people with highly empathetic leaders reported being

consistently engaged, compared to just 32% who experienced less empathy.
- **Retention:** When leaders were perceived as empathetic, only 14% of women of color and 17% of white women reported considering leaving their companies, compared to massive majorities in environments lacking empathy.

The numbers do not lie. When employees feel that a boss truly cares about them as a whole person, their loyalty and output skyrocket.

We are facing a massive generational transition. The most experienced cohort in the workforce is retiring and walking out the door with invaluable institutional knowledge, while incoming generations are demanding a new standard of authentic communication. The companies that survive this transition will not be the ones with the best software or the most ruthless management tactics. They will be the companies led by people who know how to look at their team and see the human beings standing right in front of them.

Now that we understand the biological necessity and the immense financial ROI of uncovering an employee's drive, it's time to learn how to categorize what we find.

Let's meet the Five "Why" Archetypes.

Part 3: The Five "Why" Archetypes

Chapter 5: The Five "Why" Archetypes: An Introduction

At the end of the last chapter, you became an archeologist. You now have a toolkit to carefully unearth the clues to your employees' motivations— the shards of their high-point stories, the maps of their career journeys, the dust brushed away by curious questions. You likely have a table in your mind covered with these valuable, fragmented pieces.

But a collection of shards is not a story. To make sense of what you've found, you need a framework. You need a way to see how the pieces fit together to form a recognizable shape.

This is the role of the "Why Archetypes". They are the five fundamental patterns of human motivation that I have observed again and again in my work. They are the reference guide an archeologist uses to identify if they've found a piece of a vase, a shield, or a crown. They provide a language for what you are seeing and a map for what to do next.

Think about the sheer relief and pride you feel the moment you cross a major task off your to-do list. That profound feeling of accomplishment we get after a job well done isn't just a fleeting emotion; it is our brain's natural reward system in action.

Scientifically, this is often linked to dopamine, a neurotransmitter that plays a major role in reward-motivated behavior. Dopamine signals not just pleasure, but the anticipation of a reward. When we achieve a goal that aligns with our internal drivers, our brain releases dopamine, reinforcing that behavior and making us want to do it again.

But here is the critical insight that most leaders miss: the definition of that satisfaction—the trigger for that dopamine release—differs dramatically between each individual. What one person finds deeply fulfilling, another finds tedious. The "satisfaction aftermath" that energizes one person can completely drain another.

The Five "Why" Archetypes are, in essence, five different answers to the question, "What kind of work provides your greatest sense of fulfillment?". Each archetype is wired to get that powerful feeling of accomplishment from a different kind of effort. As a leader, your job is to stop offering a generic, one-size-fits-all approach and start understanding the specific source of fulfillment that energizes each person on your team.

The Rules of the Road: Lenses, Not Labels

Before we explore these different sources of fulfillment, we must establish the ground rules for using this framework. If you ignore these, you risk turning a powerful tool for connection into a clumsy tool for division.

Rule #1: These are Lenses, Not Labels. The archetypes are not rigid boxes. They are five different lenses you can look through to better understand a person's motivations.

Rule #2: Everyone is a Blend. Almost no one is 100% a single archetype. Most people have a dominant archetype and a secondary one that gives their "Why" a unique flavor.

Rule #3: Your Role is Facilitator, Not Oracle. Your job is not to diagnose your employees and deliver a verdict. A much more powerful approach is to share the framework itself with your team and facilitate a conversation where people self-identify.

Rule #4: Archetypes are Fluid, Not Fixed. This is perhaps the most vital rule to remember. A person's dominant "Why" is not written in stone. It can and will fluctuate based on their environment, the specific task, and major life events.

We are whole humans, and our professional drives are deeply impacted by our personal realities. If an employee has just experienced a massive life transition—perhaps they just had a new baby, moved across the country, or are navigating a personal crisis—their world is inherently chaotic. During that season, even the most adventurous, risk-taking Pioneer might temporarily crave the predictability and routine of a Stabilizer at work just to keep their head above water.

Conversely, an environment can suppress a natural "Why". A brilliant Teacher placed under a highly toxic, fiercely competitive boss might suddenly start hoarding information to protect their job, completely burying their natural drive to mentor.

Your job as a leader is to watch for these situational cues, not just decide what someone is and permanently brand them with a static label. You are reading a dynamic human being, not a snapshot.

Spotting Your Own Why: The Assessment Tease

In the coming chapters, we are going to do a deep dive into each of the five archetypes. But before we look at your team, let's look at you. Which of these fundamentally drives your professional energy?

Pay attention to your gut reaction as you read these:

- **If taking a blank canvas, rolling up your sleeves, and turning an abstract idea into a tangible, finished product lights you up...** you may be a **Builder**.
- **If bringing people together, bridging communication gaps, and fostering deep team harmony lights you up...** you may be a **Connector**.
- **If seeing the "aha!" moment in someone else's eyes after you've mentored them or shared your expertise lights you up...** you may be a **Teacher**.

- **If diving headfirst into an ambiguous problem, questioning the status quo, and exploring the absolute edge of what is possible lights you up...** you may be a **Pioneer**.
- **If bringing order, streamlined process, and rock-solid predictability to a chaotic timeline lights you up...** you may be a **Stabilizer**.

While these clues will point you in the right direction, human motivation is rarely simple. Most of us are a unique, nuanced blend of these archetypes, and as we just learned, those blends can shift.

To get your exact baseline, discover your dominant and secondary drivers, and receive a customized breakdown of your motivational profile, take the official **Why Type Assessment** at meaganhopper.com/assessment.

The Power of a Shared Language

Understanding these patterns isn't just an interesting psychological exercise; it's a powerful tool for solving the most common and frustrating team conflicts.

A Story from the Wild: The Pioneer and the Stabilizer A marketing manager, Anna, was leading a website redesign project. Her two key players were Chloe, a brilliant designer, and David, a meticulous project manager. The project was a disaster.

Chloe, a Pioneer, was constantly coming up with new ideas. David, a Stabilizer, was growing increasingly frustrated that they couldn't lock down a final plan.

Instead of telling them to "just get along," Anna reframed their roles based on their archetypes. She tasked Chloe with two weeks of pure exploration and David with building the rock-solid project plan to execute the final chosen design.

The tension vanished. Understanding their archetypes didn't change the people, but it completely changed Anna's leadership strategy. She didn't just solve a conflict; she put both of her people in a position to do their best work.

This is the power you now have. You have the framework to not only understand your people but to unlock their highest potential. Now that you have the map of the framework, let's explore our first territory. It's time to meet The Builder.

Chapter 6: The Builder - The Drive to Create

There is a unique and deeply satisfying feeling that comes from looking at a finished object—the newly painted deck, the humming server, the crisp, printed pages of a final report—and thinking to yourself, "I built this." This feeling is the native language of the Builder.

The Builder archetype is driven by one of the most primal forms of human contribution: the need to bring something new and tangible into existence. They are the people who turn abstract ideas into concrete reality. They are not content to live in the world of theory; their purpose is found in the act of making, creating, and finishing.

For a Builder, progress isn't real until you can see it, touch it, or use it. They are the engines of creation on any team, and understanding their drive is the key to unlocking their incredible potential.

How to Spot a Builder

Builders often reveal themselves through their actions, language, and even their hobbies. As you start looking through this lens, you will begin to see them clearly.

- **In Their Stories:** When you ask a Builder about a "peak moment," the hero of their story is almost always the finished product.

They will light up when they talk about the time they launched a new feature, created a new system from scratch, or finished a major project ahead of schedule.

- **In Their Language:** They speak in active, tangible verbs. Listen for words like "make," "build," "produce," "ship," and "finish." In meetings, they are the ones who get restless with endless discussion and are most likely to ask, "So, what's the deliverable here?" or "What's a concrete next step?"
- **In Their Hobbies:** The Builder's drive doesn't stop at 5 p.m. Look for the employee who spends their weekends on creative, hands-on projects: woodworking, coding a personal app, knitting, gardening, home renovation, or even building complex Lego sets. Anything that results in a finished object is a powerful clue.
- **In Their Workspace:** Their desk or digital desktop is often a space of "productive chaos." It might be covered in sketches, prototypes, half-finished models, or multiple open files for a project they are actively creating. It's the visible evidence of their work-in-progress.

The Shadow Side of the Builder

While a healthy Builder is the engine of your team, a stressed, burnt-out, or misaligned Builder can quickly derail a project. When their drive to create is thwarted or put under immense pressure, you will likely see two distinct "shadow" behaviors emerge:

1. The Territorial Bottleneck When a Builder feels a lack of control or trust, they often stop collaborating entirely. Their mindset shifts to, "If I want it built right, I have to build it myself." They become fiercely territorial over their projects, refusing to delegate even minor tasks. While their work ethic might look impressive on the surface, they are actually suffocating the rest of the team and becoming a massive bottleneck that slows down the entire operation.

2. The Feature Creeper A Builder's dopamine comes from the act of making. If a project lacks clear boundaries, a Builder might just keep building to stay in that fulfilling "creation zone." They will add new features, tweak designs endlessly, and overcomplicate the deliverable long after it has met the business requirements. They prioritize the joy of building over the necessity of finishing.

Diagnosing these shadow behaviors allows you to intervene effectively. A territorial Builder doesn't need a lecture on teamwork; they need a designated piece of the project they can wholly own. A feature-creeping Builder doesn't need to be micromanaged; they need a firmer, clearer finish line.

The Builder's Language: Resonant vs. Trigger Words

Your words are a powerful tool for connecting with a Builder. Using the right language can feel like a key turning in a lock, while the wrong language can shut them down instantly.

Words that Resonate (Energize): These words signal action, ownership, and creation.

- "Let's *build* it."
- "I want you to *own this from start to finish*."
- "Here's a *blank canvas*."
- "What's a *tangible first step* we can take right now?"

Words that Trigger (Drain): These words signal inaction, bureaucracy, and futility.

- "Let's *circle back* on that for a few weeks." *(Why it triggers: It feels like a delay tactic, the opposite of progress.)*
- "We're in a phase of *analysis paralysis*." *(Why it triggers: It's their personal nightmare—all talk, no action.)*
- "Your job is just to *maintain the existing system*." *(Why it triggers: Maintenance is the absence of creation.)*

The Ideal Environment

To thrive, a Builder doesn't need much, but what they need is non-negotiable. They flourish in an environment with:

- **A Bias for Action:** A culture that values shipping and execution over endless deliberation.
- **Clear Goals:** They need a well-defined finish line. They don't mind ambiguity in *how* they get there, but they need to know *what* they are building.
- **Tangible Milestones:** They are motivated by seeing progress. Breaking a large project into smaller, deliverable chunks is a great way to keep their energy high.
- **Autonomy:** They need the freedom to figure out the best way to build. Micromanaging a Builder's process is one of the fastest ways to demotivate them.

Scaling the Framework: Builders in the Wild

Whether managing a localized social media campaign or overseeing hundreds of millions of dollars in hard assets, the fundamental drive of the Builder remains exactly the same. Here is what it looks like at both ends of the spectrum.

The Micro Scale: The Trapped Marketer Elena, a marketing director, had a classic Builder on her team named Julian. He was competent but miserable in a role that required him to simply manage the ongoing social media calendar. It was a maintenance job—the same tasks repeated every week. His metrics were good, but his energy was flat, and Elena could see he was a flight risk.

During a "Why" conversation, Elena discovered that Julian's proudest past accomplishment was launching his university's first-ever alumni podcast from scratch. Recognizing his Builder drive, she made a strategic change. She told him, "Julian, I want you to build our company's first-ever video series for a new product launch. You own it—the concept, the production, the launch plan. It's a blank canvas."

Julian's energy and performance skyrocketed. He wasn't just managing posts anymore; he was *creating an asset*. Elena didn't change his job title, but by tailoring the work to his Builder drive, she transformed his job into a calling.

The Macro Scale: The $250 Million Bottleneck
The stakes change, but the psychology doesn't. Consider Robert, a VP of Development overseeing a massive, highly visible $250 million commercial construction project. Robert cut his teeth in the industry as a brilliant field engineer; he was a Builder to his core.

But as the VP, his calendar was entirely consumed by managing nervous investors (Connector work) and reviewing endless compliance and risk-mitigation audits (Stabilizer work). He was exhausted, operating deep in his shadow side, and the project timeline was starting to slip. He was trying to muscle through by working 80-hour weeks, but he was starving for the satisfaction of actual creation.

The intervention wasn't to give Robert a pep talk; it was structural. The executive team paired Robert with a highly capable Deputy Director whose dominant archetypes were Stabilizer and Connector. They explicitly tasked the Deputy with handling the red tape, the reporting, and the stakeholder pacification.

This unleashed Robert. He was freed to get his boots back in the dirt. He spent his days walking the site, solving physical design clashes, and driving the critical path of the actual build. By realigning his macro-role with his internal drive to see the steel rise, his burnout vanished, and the project got back on schedule.

Builder Dynamics: How They Interact with Other Archetypes

- **With a Connector:** This is a powerful pairing for launching a new product. The Builder can be heads-down, focused on creating the best possible product. The Connector can be outward-facing, managing stakeholder expectations, gathering customer feedback, and ensuring the team is communicating effectively.
- **With a Teacher:** Another strong synergy. The Builder creates the new system, and the Teacher creates the documentation and training that ensures everyone can use it effectively.

- **With a Pioneer:** This is the classic "dream it, build it" duo. The Pioneer comes up with the groundbreaking, never-been-done-before idea, and the Builder figures out how to turn that wild vision into a functional prototype.
- **With a Stabilizer:** This can be a source of productive tension or outright conflict. The Builder wants to build it *now*. The Stabilizer wants to build it *right*, with a perfect plan. The leader's job is to sequence their work. Task the Builder with creating the V1 prototype quickly. Then, task the Stabilizer with turning that prototype into a scalable, bulletproof, V2 process.

Spotting the Blends: The Nuance of the Builder

Look for these common combinations to understand the unique flavor of the Builders on your team:

- **The Builder-Teacher:** This person doesn't just want to build the new system; they want to write the user manual, create the "how-to" videos, and lead the training workshop. They find joy in creating something and then empowering others with their creation.
- **The Builder-Stabilizer:** This is your master craftsperson. They don't just want to build it fast; they want to build it *perfectly*, with clean code, elegant processes, and an eye toward long-term quality and reliability. For them, the beauty is not just in the finished

product, but in the quality of its construction.

- **The Builder-Pioneer:** This is the "Innovator." They aren't interested in building the same old thing; they are driven to build the *new* thing. They are obsessed with using new tools, technologies, and methods to create something that has never existed before.

Chapter 7: The Connector - The Drive to Unify

Think about the best team you've ever been a part of. Not just a group of people who worked on the same project, but a true team. A team where you felt a sense of belonging, where communication was easy, and where you trusted your colleagues implicitly. More likely than not, there was a Connector at the heart of that experience.

The Connector archetype is driven by the fundamental human need for community. They are the weavers of the social fabric in any organization. While others might focus on the tasks, the product, or the process, the Connector is instinctively focused on the *people*. They understand that the quality of the relationships determines the quality of the work.

For them, a project's success is not just measured by the final result, but by *how* the team felt while achieving it. They are the empathetic heart of any team, and their ability to build bridges is a true superpower.

How to Spot a Connector

Connectors are often easy to spot because their "Why" is so outwardly focused. They reveal themselves through their collaborative nature and their investment in the well-being of the group.

- **In Their Stories:** When you ask a Connector about a "peak moment," the story will almost always be full of "we," not "I". They will talk enthusiastically about a time the team "just clicked," a successful collaborative project, or the satisfaction of winning over a difficult client and building a strong, trusting relationship.
- **In Their Language:** They are natural diplomats. Listen for words like "collaboration," "team win," "alignment," "rapport," and "community". In meetings, they are often the ones who notice if someone is being quiet and will actively solicit their opinion: "Maya, we haven't heard from you yet, what are your thoughts on this?".
- **In Their Hobbies:** Connectors often gravitate toward group activities. They might be part of a sports league, a book club, or a volunteer organization. They are often the designated planner in their friend group, organizing the trips and gatherings that keep everyone in touch.
- **In Their Daily Actions:** They are the "culture carriers". They are the ones who remember birthdays, organize the team lunches, and are the first to welcome a new hire and make them feel like part of the group.

The Shadow Side of the Connector

Because a Connector's energy is derived from harmony and relationship-building, a toxic environment or an overwhelming workload can turn their greatest strengths into heavy liabilities. When a Connector is operating in their "shadow side," you will typically see two distinct behaviors:

1. The People-Pleasing Martyr When a team is under extreme stress, a Connector will desperately try to keep the peace. In doing so, they often abandon their own boundaries. They will say "yes" to every request to avoid disappointing anyone, taking on an unsustainable workload. Worse, to maintain superficial harmony, they will avoid having necessary, difficult conversations. They become a "peacekeeper" rather than a "peacemaker," allowing toxic behaviors from others to go unchecked because they are terrified of conflict.

2. Compassion Fatigue Because Connectors are naturally empathetic and serve as the emotional sounding board for the team, they are highly susceptible to absorbing everyone else's stress. If the organizational culture is negative, the Connector becomes the dumping ground for the team's complaints. Without proper boundaries or a leader who protects their energy, the Connector will eventually burn out from the sheer weight of carrying the emotional baggage of the entire department. They will suddenly withdraw, becoming cynical and emotionally unavailable—a stark contrast to their usual vibrant selves.

The Connector's Language: Resonant vs. Trigger Words

Connecting with this archetype is about using inclusive, team-focused language.

Words that Resonate (Energize): These words signal collaboration, empathy, and shared purpose.

- "*We* need to solve this *together*."
- "I need you to *build a strong relationship* with this client."
- "Let's make sure we get *everyone aligned* on this."
- "The most important thing is that the *team feels supported*."

Words that Trigger (Drain): These words signal isolation, competition, and a lack of psychological safety.

- "Just stay in your lane and focus on *your task*." *(Why it triggers: It denies their need for collaboration and a holistic view.)*
- "This is on a *need-to-know basis*." *(Why it triggers: It creates information silos and breaks down trust.)*
- "It's an *every-person-for-themselves* project." *(Why it triggers: It's the polar opposite of their core drive.)*

The Ideal Environment

A Connector's energy is directly tied to the health of their social environment. They thrive in a culture that values:

- **Psychological Safety:** An environment where people feel safe to speak up, share ideas, and be vulnerable.
- **Collaboration:** Clear opportunities for teamwork and cross-functional projects.
- **Transparency:** Open and honest communication from leadership and across the team.
- **A Focus on People:** A culture that recognizes and celebrates team wins, not just individual heroics.

Scaling the Framework: Connectors in the Wild

The Connector's ability to unify is just as crucial for a five-person task force as it is for a global enterprise.

The Micro Scale: The Empathic Engineer An engineering team was struggling. The coders were brilliant, but they were mostly Builders and Pioneers who disliked the "people work" of constant meetings. As a result, they worked in silos, and there was constant friction with the product management team, leading to missed deadlines. Their manager, Alex, realized he was asking his best Builders to do Connector work, and it was draining their energy.

During this time, Alex identified one of his senior engineers, Maya, as a natural Connector. While she was a great coder, her real gift was her empathy and ability to build rapport. She was the one everyone went to for advice.

Instead of just adding more work to her plate, Alex made a bold strategic move. He called Maya into his office and offered her a new, formal position: "Principal Engineer, Product Liaison". Her primary responsibility would no longer be writing code, but managing the flow of communication between the engineering and product teams. She would sit in on planning meetings, translate requirements, and be the human bridge between the two worlds.

The change was transformative. Maya thrived, energized by a role that perfectly matched her "Why". The other engineers were visibly relieved; freed from the communication overhead they disliked, their meeting load decreased and they could focus on the deep, creative work they loved. Their productivity soared. The friction between the teams vanished. Alex didn't hire a new person; he unlocked the potential of his entire team by formally recognizing and activating the Connector "Why" that was already there.

The Macro Scale: The Post-Merger Peacemaker
When a mid-sized tech firm was acquired by a massive corporate conglomerate, the executive team prepared for the usual challenges: software integration, budget alignment, and real estate

consolidation. What they didn't anticipate was the toxic, hostile culture war that erupted. The legacy employees felt completely alienated, and the acquiring company's staff viewed the new additions with suspicion. Turnover spiked, and productivity tanked.

The CEO, Daniel, realized that all the project management in the world couldn't fix a broken social fabric. He pulled Rachel, a VP of Operations with a dominant Connector archetype, off her standard duties and gave her a new mandate. She became the "Integration Czar"—but her focus wasn't on software. It was entirely on the *people*.

Rachel immediately set up cross-company "listening tours." She paired legacy leaders with new leaders for low-stakes collaborative projects to force relationship-building. She created safe, transparent forums for employees to voice their anxieties without fear of retaliation. Because Rachel's intrinsic drive was to create unity, she had the patience and empathy to untangle the emotional knots that the rest of the executive team wanted to ignore. Within six months, the "us vs. them" mentality dissolved, saving the company millions in potential turnover costs.

Connector Dynamics: How They Interact with Other Archetypes

- **With a Builder:** The ideal product-launch duo. The Builder focuses on making the best possible "what," while the Connector focuses on the "who"—the team building it and the customers who will use it.

- **With a Teacher:** A powerful combination for building a mentoring culture. The Teacher has the expertise, and the Connector creates the safe, trusting relationships that make mentorship effective.
- **With a Pioneer:** The Connector can be the Pioneer's "ground control". The Pioneer can get lost in their world of ideas, and the Connector can help them bring those ideas back to the team, build consensus, and ensure their innovative work gets the support it needs.
- **With a Stabilizer:** This pairing creates highly effective, happy teams. The Stabilizer builds the clear, reliable processes, and the Connector ensures the team feels good about using them, creating a culture of both efficiency and high morale.

Spotting the Blends: The Nuance of the Connector

- **The Connector-Teacher:** This is your natural team lead or culture champion. They not only want the team to work well together, but they are also driven to actively teach them *how* to do it, leading workshops on communication or mentoring others on collaboration.

- **The Connector-Stabilizer:** This is the ultimate project manager. They are masters of both the "people" and the "plan". They can create a rock-solid project timeline while also masterfully managing stakeholder relationships and team morale.
- **The Connector-Builder:** This person is passionate about building communities. They are not just interested in creating a product; they are interested in creating the user group, the fan club, and the entire ecosystem of relationships around that product.

Chapter 8: The Teacher - The Drive to Mentor

There is a distinct, almost electric moment that happens when you are explaining a complex concept to someone, and you see their eyes suddenly widen. It's the "aha!" moment. The exact second when confusion gives way to clarity.

For most people, that moment is nice to witness. For a Teacher, that moment is the ultimate professional reward.

The Teacher archetype is driven by the transfer of knowledge. They are the mentors, the guides, and the subject-matter experts who find their deepest fulfillment in elevating the competence of the people around them. They do not want to simply hold the answers; they want to build the capacity of others to find the answers themselves.

If the Builder is driven to create the product, the Teacher is driven to cultivate the *person*. They are the institutional memory of your organization and the key to scaling your team's capabilities.

How to Spot a Teacher

Teachers often naturally gravitate toward the front of the room, even if they don't have a formal leadership title.

- **In Their Stories:** Their "peak moments" rarely center on their own solo accomplishments. Instead, they will proudly tell you about the time a junior employee they were mentoring finally mastered a difficult skill, or the time they designed a training manual that the whole department now uses. Their wins are almost always reflected in the success of others.
- **In Their Language:** They use words associated with growth and clarity. Listen for "framework," "methodology," "onboarding," "upskill," and "guide." In meetings, if someone asks a question, the Teacher won't just give a yes-or-no answer; they will instinctively provide the context and the *why* behind the answer.
- **In Their Hobbies:** Their drive to mentor frequently bleeds into their personal lives. They are the youth sports coaches, the weekend tutors, the adjunct professors, or the people hosting free workshops in their community.
- **In Their Daily Actions:** They are the ones who voluntarily create the "How-To" documents for the software no one understands. They are the first to volunteer to train the new hire.

The Shadow Side of the Teacher

A healthy Teacher multiplies the intelligence of your team. But when a Teacher feels threatened, undervalued, or insecure in their position, their drive can twist into highly destructive behaviors.

1. The Knowledge Hoarder This is the most dangerous shadow side of the Teacher. If they feel that their expertise is the only thing keeping them employed—if there is no psychological safety— they will stop teaching. Instead, they will hoard information to make themselves utterly indispensable. They become a "black box" where data goes in, but the process never comes out. They weaponize their expertise, doling out answers slowly and refusing to document their processes, crippling the team's ability to operate without them.

2. The Unsolicited Critic (The Micromanager) When a Teacher doesn't have an appropriate outlet for their drive, they will force "teaching moments" where none are needed. They will micromanage the *how* of a project, constantly correcting their peers on minor, stylistic details under the guise of "just trying to help you improve." They become pedantic, slowing down progress because they can't let anyone do a task differently than they would do it themselves.

The Teacher's Language: Resonant vs. Trigger Words

To activate a Teacher, you must validate their expertise and give them the platform to share it.

Words that Resonate (Energize): * "Can you *show the team how* you did this?"

- "I'd love for you to *mentor* the new hires."
- "Can you help me *build a framework* for this process?"
- "Your *expertise* on this is invaluable."

Words that Trigger (Drain): * "Just give me the answer, *skip the explanation." (Why it triggers: The explanation is the entire point for them.)*

- "Keep your methods *to yourself." (Why it triggers: It actively shuts down their core drive to share.)*
- "We don't have time for *training." (Why it triggers: It devalues the long-term growth they prioritize.)*

The Ideal Environment

A Teacher needs an environment that respects mastery and allows for the time required to transfer knowledge. They thrive with:

- **Opportunities for Mentorship:** Formal or informal programs where they can guide others.
- **Respect for Expertise:** A culture that values deep knowledge, not just quick, superficial execution.
- **Time for Documentation:** They need leadership to acknowledge that creating a

training guide or documenting a process is "real work" that takes time, not just an administrative afterthought.

Scaling the Framework: Teachers in the Wild

The drive to elevate others scales perfectly from small, intimate teams to massive, enterprise-wide deployments.

The Micro Scale: The Frustrated Designer Sam was a senior graphic designer at a boutique marketing agency. He was incredibly talented, but lately, he had become cynical and short-tempered. His manager noticed he was flying through his design work but seemed entirely disengaged.

During a 1-on-1, Sam admitted he was bored. "I'm just churning out assets," he said. "I could do this in my sleep." His manager realized Sam had mastered his role, but instead of promoting him to an administrative "Art Director" role (which Sam didn't want), she tapped into his Teacher archetype.

She asked Sam to run a bi-weekly "Lunch and Learn" for the junior designers, giving him two hours a week to prepare a curriculum on advanced design theory and software shortcuts. The transformation was immediate. Sam's cynicism vanished. He poured his energy into creating brilliant presentations, and the quality of the junior designers' work skyrocketed. Sam found his purpose again, not by doing *more* work, but by *sharing* how he worked.

The Macro Scale: The Global Rollout Marcus was the Director of Operations for a logistics company with 500 employees. The company was about to undergo a massive, highly disruptive transition to a new Enterprise Resource Planning (ERP) software system. Marcus was tapped to manage the vendor contracts and the budget—pure Stabilizer work.

Within a month, Marcus was miserable. He was buried in spreadsheets and legally dense contracts. Meanwhile, the frontline employees were panicking about the new software, and morale was plummeting.

The executive team realized they had misdiagnosed Marcus. He wasn't a Stabilizer; he was a Teacher. They immediately pivoted his role. They handed the vendor contracts to a financial controller and put Marcus in charge of the Global Change Management and Training Rollout.

Marcus came alive. He spent the next six months designing comprehensive training modules, flying to regional offices to host town halls, and training a small army of internal "Super Users" to act as local guides. He turned a terrifying, chaotic software rollout into an empowering masterclass for 500 people. Because he was operating in his Teacher

"Why," the adoption rate of the new software was virtually flawless.

Teacher Dynamics: How They Interact with Other Archetypes

- **With a Pioneer:** The Pioneer dreams up the completely new, never-before-seen process, and the Teacher figures out how to explain it so the rest of the company can actually understand and adopt it.
- **With a Stabilizer:** A Stabilizer loves a good standard operating procedure (SOP), and the Teacher loves to write them. Together, they can build incredibly robust, scalable training programs.
- **With a Builder:** The Builder creates the software, and the Teacher writes the user manual. They are a natural pair for product launches.

Spotting the Blends: The Nuance of the Teacher

- **The Teacher-Pioneer:** This is the "Thought Leader." They don't want to teach the old, established methods. They are driven to discover cutting-edge theories and be the first to teach them to the industry.
- **The Teacher-Connector:** The ultimate facilitator. They excel in group learning environments, workshops, and retreats. They are just as focused on building a supportive

community among the students as they are on the curriculum itself.

- **The Teacher-Stabilizer:** The "Compliance Master." They are driven to teach the rules, the safety protocols, and the exact step-by-step processes to ensure everything runs perfectly and safely.

Chapter 9: The Pioneer - The Drive to Explore

There is a certain type of person who looks at a perfectly functioning system, tilts their head, and asks, "But what if we did it entirely differently?"

This is the Pioneer.

If the Stabilizer's nightmare is a lack of process, the Pioneer's nightmare is the phrase, "Because that's how we've always done it." The Pioneer archetype is driven by the thrill of the unknown, the pursuit of innovation, and the desire to push past the established boundaries of what is possible. They are the visionaries, the disruptors, and the early adopters.

While a Builder gets their dopamine from finishing a product, a Pioneer gets their dopamine from the *discovery* of the idea itself. They thrive in ambiguity. When the path forward is unclear and there is no manual to follow, the Pioneer doesn't feel anxiety; they feel exhilaration. They are the vanguard of your team, essential for keeping your company from stagnating in a rapidly changing world.

How to Spot a Pioneer

Pioneers are often the most vocal people in a brainstorming session, constantly throwing out "what if" scenarios.

- **In Their Stories:** When you ask a Pioneer about a peak moment, they will talk about the time they had to figure something out from scratch. They love telling stories about breaking the mold, proving a skeptic wrong, or successfully launching a wild, experimental initiative that no one else thought would work.
- **In Their Language:** They speak in the future tense and use words of possibility. Listen for "disrupt," "innovate," "explore," "reimagine," and "what if." They are quick to use metaphors and love to talk about the "big picture" rather than the granular details.
- **In Their Hobbies:** Look for the person who is always picking up a new, obscure hobby, traveling to off-the-beaten-path destinations, or beta-testing the newest, unreleased app. They are driven by novelty and exploration in all areas of their life.
- **In Their Daily Actions:** They are the first to volunteer for the messy, undefined projects. If there is a sudden crisis or a completely unprecedented challenge, the Pioneer is the one who steps forward while everyone else takes a step back.

The Shadow Side of the Pioneer

Because the Pioneer's energy is derived from novelty and ideation, they can struggle deeply with execution and routine. When mismanaged, unmotivated, or left unchecked, their drive to explore can create chaos for the rest of the team.

1. Shiny Object Syndrome This is the classic Pioneer shadow behavior. They love the first 10% of a project—the brainstorming, the strategy, the exciting kickoff. But once the project moves into the predictable, repetitive phase of execution (the middle 80%), they lose all their dopamine. They become bored and immediately start looking for the next "shiny object" or new initiative to launch, abandoning their current projects halfway through and leaving a trail of unfinished work for the rest of the team to clean up.

2. The Chaotic Disruptor When a Pioneer feels constrained by too much bureaucracy, they might start breaking rules just to feel a sense of autonomy. They will change established processes, introduce untested software, or pivot team strategies on a whim without consulting anyone. They justify this as "innovation," but to the rest of the team— especially the Stabilizers—it is just exhausting, unpredictable chaos that destroys productivity.

The Pioneer's Language: Resonant vs. Trigger Words

To activate a Pioneer, you have to give them permission to think outside the box and challenge the status quo.

Words that Resonate (Energize): * "I want you to *explore* some completely new options."

- "There are *no rules* for this brainstorming session."
- "We need to *reimagine* how we approach this."
- "What is the most *innovative* way we could solve this?"

Words that Trigger (Drain): * "Just *follow the manual* exactly as it's written." *(Why it triggers: It completely removes their autonomy and creativity.)*

- "We can't do that; *it's too risky.*" *(Why it triggers: They view risk as a necessary ingredient for progress.)*
- "Let's stick to the *tried-and-true* method." *(Why it triggers: It guarantees stagnation, which is their ultimate fear.)*

The Ideal Environment

A Pioneer will suffocate in an environment built entirely on rigid compliance. They need:

- **High Autonomy:** They need the freedom to experiment, fail, and try again without being micromanaged.
- **Tolerance for Ambiguity:** A culture that doesn't demand perfect answers immediately, but allows for a period of exploration.

- **A Sandbox:** They need a safe space—a specific project or a designated amount of time—where they are explicitly allowed to test wild ideas without jeopardizing the core business operations.

Scaling the Framework: Pioneers in the Wild

The Pioneer's drive to explore is essential for overcoming stagnation, whether in a single department or across a global brand.

The Micro Scale: The Bored Analyst Tariq was a brilliant data analyst at a financial firm. He was hired to run the weekly performance reports. For the first two months, he was a superstar, completely redesigning the report templates. But by month six, he was constantly missing deadlines and making careless copy-paste errors. His manager assumed Tariq had lost his work ethic.

During a "Why" conversation, Tariq revealed his peak moment: the time he had taught himself a new programming language just to see if he could automate a cumbersome data pull. His manager realized Tariq wasn't lazy; he was a Pioneer dying of boredom. Running the same report every Friday offered zero novelty.

His manager made a simple pivot. She kept Tariq on the weekly reports but gave him a "Pioneer Sandbox": every Thursday afternoon was strictly reserved for Tariq to experiment with new predictive modeling software the company was considering. Giving him just four hours a week of pure exploration completely reignited his engagement, and the careless errors on his Friday reports vanished.

The Macro Scale: The Entertainment Executive
Consider Nadia, the VP of Guest Experience for a massive, globally recognized theme park and entertainment brand. She managed a team of thousands. Historically, her role had been treated as a Stabilizer position—focused entirely on minimizing wait times, ensuring safety compliance, and maintaining the operational status quo.

But Nadia was a Pioneer. She wasn't interested in making the current line move 5% faster; she wanted to know why people were waiting in lines at all. She felt constrained by the legacy thinking of the organization and was considering leaving for a nimble tech startup.

The CEO recognized her drive and fundamentally changed her mandate. He pulled her out of the day-to-day operational compliance (handing that to a true Stabilizer) and tasked Nadia with building the "Guest Experience of 2035." He gave her a dedicated R&D budget and told her to reimagine everything from ticketing to immersive, in-park technology.

Unleashed in her natural Pioneer environment, Nadia thrived. She spearheaded the development of wearable technology that eliminated physical lines entirely—a massive, disruptive innovation that revolutionized the industry and drove unprecedented revenue for the company.

Pioneer Dynamics: How They Interact with Other Archetypes

- **With a Stabilizer:** This is the most fraught, yet most necessary, pairing. The Pioneer creates the chaos of innovation; the Stabilizer creates the order of execution. If they don't understand each other's "Why," they will go to war. If they do, they are unstoppable.
- **With a Builder:** A highly effective pair. The Pioneer says, "What if we built a flying car?" and the Builder figures out how to actually construct the engine.
- **With a Connector:** The Connector acts as the Pioneer's translator. Pioneers can sometimes alienate people with their radical ideas. The Connector helps build consensus and brings the rest of the team on board with the Pioneer's vision.

Spotting the Blends: The Nuance of the Pioneer

- **The Pioneer-Builder:** The "Inventor." They don't just want to theorize about the future; they want to physically build the prototype of the future.

- **The Pioneer-Teacher:** The "Evangelist."
  They discover the new, cutting-edge method
  and immediately want to host a masterclass
  to teach the rest of the industry how to do it.
- **The Pioneer-Connector:** The "Networker."
  They explore by connecting with people.
  They are constantly seeking out thought
  leaders, attending avant-garde conferences,
  and bringing diverse groups of people
  together to spark new, disruptive ideas.

Chapter 10: The Stabilizer - The Drive to Create Order

Imagine walking into a room where papers are scattered everywhere, the fire alarm is faintly beeping, and three different people are shouting conflicting instructions. For most of the archetypes, this is a nightmare. For a Pioneer, it might be an exciting challenge.

But for a Stabilizer, it is a visceral, biological mandate to intervene and create order.

The Stabilizer archetype is driven by the need for predictability, consistency, and structure. They are the architects of process and the mitigators of risk. While the Pioneer asks, "What if we change everything?" the Stabilizer asks, "What is the backup plan if this breaks?"

They do not get their dopamine from breaking the rules; they get their dopamine from writing the rules so that everyone else can succeed safely and efficiently. They are the bedrock of your organization. Without Stabilizers, a company might have brilliant ideas, but it will never be able to scale them.

How to Spot a Stabilizer

Stabilizers are the quiet heroes of the operational world. They are often the ones catching the mistakes everyone else missed.

- **In Their Stories:** When you ask a Stabilizer about a peak moment, they will rarely talk about being in the spotlight. Instead, they will proudly tell you about the time they successfully audited a failing department, streamlined a chaotic onboarding process, or anticipated a massive crisis and had the contingency plan ready to go before anyone else even noticed the threat.
- **In Their Language:** They speak the language of logistics and risk. Listen for words like "process," "efficiency," "contingency," "standardize," and "timeline." In meetings, they are the ones asking the practical, grounding questions: "Who is maintaining this after launch?" or "Have we budgeted for the maintenance phase?"
- **In Their Hobbies:** Their drive for order often extends into their personal lives. They might be avid collectors, meticulous budgeters, or the friends who build out the incredibly detailed, color-coded itineraries for group vacations.
- **In Their Daily Actions:** Look at their digital workspace. A Stabilizer's inbox is often at "Inbox Zero," their calendar is impeccably managed, and they are the undisputed masters of the spreadsheet. They find deep satisfaction in a perfectly formatted cell.

The Shadow Side of the Stabilizer

Because a Stabilizer's energy is derived from predictability, an environment of constant, unmanaged chaos will trigger their deepest anxieties. When a Stabilizer feels unsafe or overwhelmed, their drive for order mutates into defensive, restrictive behaviors.

1. The Bureaucratic Bottleneck When a Stabilizer feels that things are moving too fast and recklessly, they will hit the emergency brake. They do this by weaponizing red tape. They will suddenly require three different signatures for a routine approval, demand endless rounds of testing, and refuse to move forward without absolute, 100% certainty. They aren't trying to be difficult; their nervous system is trying to protect the company from what they perceive as dangerous chaos. Unfortunately, this paralyzes the team's momentum.

2. The Change Resister A stressed Stabilizer will view any new initiative not as an opportunity, but as a threat to the established, working order. If leadership forces a new software or process on them without explaining the *why* or giving them time to prepare, the Stabilizer will dig their heels in. They will actively fight the innovation, pointing out every single flaw and reason it won't work, souring the morale of the rest of the team.

The Stabilizer's Language: Resonant vs. Trigger Words

To activate a Stabilizer, you must validate their need for structure and respect their ability to see the risks others miss.

Words that Resonate (Energize): * "I need you to build a *standard operating procedure* for this."

- "What are the *risks* we aren't seeing?"
- "Let's *lock in the timeline* and responsibilities."
- "We value your *consistency* on this project."

Words that Trigger (Drain): * "Let's just *wing it* and see what happens." *(Why it triggers: It is the literal definition of chaos and risk.)*

- "We'll *figure out the details later*." *(Why it triggers: To a Stabilizer, the details are the only thing that matters.)*
- "Just *disrupt* the whole system." *(Why it triggers: Disruption destroys the predictability they crave.)*

The Ideal Environment

A Stabilizer will quickly burn out in a startup environment that prides itself on "moving fast and breaking things" unless they are explicitly given the power to fix the broken things. They thrive with:

- **Clear Expectations:** They need to know exactly what success looks like and what the boundaries are.

- **Respect for Process:** A culture that doesn't just write SOPs, but actually follows them.
- **Time to Prepare:** They hate being caught off guard. Give them the agenda before the meeting, not during it.

Scaling the Framework: Stabilizers in the Wild

The drive to create order is just as vital for a two-person admin team as it is for managing global supply chains.

The Micro Scale: The Drowning Coordinator

Olivia was an operations coordinator at a fast-growing, highly chaotic tech startup. The founders were visionary Pioneers, which meant the company strategy changed weekly. Olivia was drowning. She was working 12-hour days just to keep the invoices paid and the lights on, constantly putting out operational fires. She was exhausted, cynical, and had a draft of her resignation letter saved on her desktop.

Her manager finally sat down and used the Archeologist's Toolkit. He realized Olivia didn't hate the company; she hated the chaos. She was a Stabilizer trapped in a reactive nightmare.

He changed her mandate. "Olivia," he said, "stop fighting the fires. I want you to build the firehouse." He explicitly empowered her to stop answering every urgent, chaotic request and instead dedicate her time to building the company's first true operating manual. He gave her the authority to enforce new intake processes for the founders' wild ideas.

By shifting her from a reactive firefighter to a proactive systems architect, her burnout vanished. She found her flow state, built a rock-solid operational foundation, and stayed with the company for five more years.

The Macro Scale: The Global Supply Chain Crisis James was a VP of Logistics for a massive retail brand. When a global shipping crisis hit—ports shutting down, materials delayed, costs skyrocketing—the executive board panicked. The Builder and Pioneer executives wanted to immediately source wild new materials or completely overhaul the product lines to compensate.

James, a dominant Stabilizer, recognized that introducing more variables into a chaotic system would only accelerate the collapse. He stepped in and demanded the exact opposite of disruption: radical predictability.

He didn't try to reinvent the supply chain; he fortified it. He built an incredibly rigorous, data-driven contingency framework. He standardized communication protocols across dozens of international vendors, mapped out secondary and tertiary backup routes for their most critical assets, and locked down strict new budget compliance rules. While competitors were flailing trying to pivot, James's drive for order created a secure, predictable bunker that allowed his company to weather the global storm with minimal losses.

Stabilizer Dynamics: How They Interact with Other Archetypes

- **With a Pioneer:** The ultimate yin and yang. The Pioneer needs the Stabilizer to turn their wild ideas into scalable reality. The Stabilizer needs the Pioneer to ensure their perfect processes don't become obsolete. When they respect each other's "Why," it is the most powerful combination in business.
- **With a Teacher:** A highly symbiotic relationship. The Stabilizer writes the perfect, risk-mitigated rules, and the Teacher creates the curriculum to ensure the entire company learns them.
- **With a Builder:** The Stabilizer ensures the Builder is constructing something that is up to code, within budget, and built to last.

Spotting the Blends: The Nuance of the Stabilizer

- **The Stabilizer-Teacher:** The "Compliance Trainer." They don't just write the safety manual; they find deep fulfillment in training the entire staff on exactly how to follow it to stay safe and efficient.

- **The Stabilizer-Connector:** The "Culture Operations Manager." They bring order to the "people" side of the business. They love building predictable, fair HR systems, creating transparent review processes, and ensuring everyone feels securely supported by the company infrastructure.
- **The Stabilizer-Builder:** The "Quality Assurance Architect." They are driven to build things, but their primary focus is on the integrity of the build. They are the ones testing the software for bugs or inspecting the construction site to ensure absolute perfection before launch.

Part 4: Leading for Purpose

Chapter 11: Tailoring the Role: Aligning Work With Why

You've done the archeological dig. You've listened to the high-point stories. You now have a solid understanding of the dominant archetypes on your team. You know who your Builders are, where your Stabilizers are hiding, and which of your people are secretly Pioneers.

Now comes the inevitable panic of the practical manager: *"What am I supposed to do with this? I can't rewrite everyone's job description. The work still has to get done."*

This is the most common misconception about purpose-driven leadership. Aligning an employee's work with their "Why" does not mean you have to go to Human Resources and completely overhaul their official role. It doesn't mean you stop assigning them the mundane, necessary tasks of the business.

It means you engage in the art of **Job Crafting**.

Job crafting is the process of slightly reshaping the boundaries, the framing, or the execution of a person's role to better align with their intrinsic drivers. You aren't changing the destination (the work still gets done); you are changing the vehicle they use to get there.

The 20% Shift

Here is the secret to immense retention and motivation: an employee does not need to spend 100% of their time operating in their dominant "Why" to feel fulfilled.

Extensive research into employee engagement and burnout, most notably by Marcus Buckingham and the ADP Research Institute, has revealed a fascinating threshold. The data shows that if an employee spends at least 20% of their time engaged in tasks they find intrinsically motivating—activities that truly light them up—their risk of burnout plummets. They become highly resilient to stress.

That 20% of highly resonant work provides the psychological fuel required to tackle the other 80% of their routine, mundane tasks.

Your goal as a leader is not to create a utopian, friction-free job. Your goal is to find that 20%.

- **For the Builder:** Can you carve out two hours a week for them to design a new template, even if their main job is data entry?
- **For the Teacher:** Can you assign them to mentor the newest intern for one afternoon a week?
- **For the Connector:** Can they be the designated liaison for a cross-departmental committee?

When you intentionally carve out this space, you stop managing their time and start managing their energy.

The Open Table Strategy: Letting Them Choose

Sometimes the best way to tailor a role is to step back and let the team do it themselves.

As a leader, you do not always need to hand down specific, granular instructions—and frankly, some archetypes strongly resent it when you do. A Pioneer or a Builder wants the autonomy to figure out the *how*.

Instead of assigning tasks top-down, try the "Open Table Strategy" at your next team meeting. When launching a new initiative with multiple moving parts, simply lay all the requirements, problems, and necessary tasks out on the table. Present the Smorgasbord of work that needs to be done, provide the ultimate deadline, and then ask the team: *"Who wants to take point on which pieces?"*

Then, watch what happens.

- The **Stabilizer** will likely gravitate toward the risk-assessment, the budgeting, or the timeline management.
- The **Pioneer** will volunteer to research the completely new software needed for the project.

- The **Teacher** will offer to document the process so they can train the rest of the department later.
- The **Connector** will offer to handle the stakeholder communication and check-ins.
- The **Builder** will immediately grab the most tangible deliverable—the prototype, the slide deck, or the code.

Giving your team the autonomy to choose their own adventure serves a dual purpose. First, it massively increases their happiness and buy-in because they selected the work themselves. Second, it serves as a brilliant, real-time diagnostic tool for you. Observing what tasks your people naturally gravitate toward when given free rein is one of the most accurate ways to verify their true "Why" archetype.

The Misdiagnosis Trap

Whether you are assigning the work or they are choosing it, we must address a critical danger zone: the Misdiagnosis Trap.

Human behavior is complex, and the actions of one archetype can often mimic the actions of another. If you simply guess your team's types based on a quick observation rather than using the Open Table strategy, having them take a formal assessment, or doing a thorough archeological dig, you will likely fall into one of these common traps.

Trap 1: The False Builder (Actually a Pioneer)
You have an employee, Kevin, who is always pitching new product ideas and loves being part of the kickoff meetings for new initiatives. You assume he is a Builder. You give him a massive, complex project to build from the ground up and tell him to "own the execution." A month later, the project is stalling.

- **The Misdiagnosis:** Kevin isn't a Builder; he is a Pioneer. He loves the idea of the product, the novelty, and the brainstorming. But he gets absolutely zero dopamine from the methodical execution required to actually build it.
- **The Fix:** Pair Kevin with a true Builder. Let Kevin pioneer the concept, then hand the blueprints to the Builder to execute.

Trap 2: The False Teacher (Actually a Stabilizer) Sofia is a senior manager who is constantly correcting the formatting on her team's reports, rewriting their emails, and sending out reminders about the company's official operating procedures. You assume she is a Teacher. You ask her to design and lead a massive, two-day training retreat for the entire division. Sofia immediately becomes stressed and overwhelmed.

- **The Misdiagnosis:** Sofia isn't correcting people because she is driven to mentor (Teacher); she is correcting people because she is terrified of risk and non-compliance

(Stabilizer). She doesn't want to stand in front of a room and inspire people; she wants everyone to follow the rules so the system doesn't break.

- **The Fix:** Cancel the training retreat. Instead, ask Sofia to audit the current onboarding manual and rewrite the compliance checklists to ensure they are foolproof.

Trap 3: The False Connector (Actually a Teacher) You notice an employee who is always holding court in the breakroom, talking to junior staff, and seemingly holding the team together socially. You assume they are a Connector and put them in charge of organizing the company's annual culture-building summit. They do a terrible job, the logistics are a mess, and they seem frustrated.

- **The Misdiagnosis:** They weren't socializing to build emotional consensus (Connector); they were holding court because they love answering questions and sharing their expertise (Teacher). They want an audience to educate, not a party to plan.

The key to avoiding the Misdiagnosis Trap is to remember that the action is just a clue; the *feeling* is the answer. Always look for the source of the dopamine.

Framing the Mundane

Even with a perfect diagnosis, a 20% shift, and the Open Table strategy, your team will still have to do things they don't want to do. The Stabilizer still has to brainstorm sometimes. The Pioneer still has to file their expense reports.

When assigning work that falls outside of an employee's dominant archetype, the secret is in the framing. You must translate the boring task into their native language.

Let's say you have to roll out a tedious new compliance software. Everyone has to take a boring two-hour certification course. Here is how you frame that exact same mundane task to the different archetypes:

- **To the Stabilizer:** "This new software is going to completely eliminate the data errors we've been having. I need you to master it so we can lock down our security."
- **To the Pioneer:** "This software is going to automate the boring stuff. If we get this certification out of the way, it frees up our bandwidth to experiment with that new project we talked about."
- **To the Connector:** "The rest of the team is really struggling with this transition. If we can get certified quickly, we can help carry the load for the others and keep the morale up."
- **To the Teacher:** "I need someone to become the absolute master of this new

software so you can be the go-to resource when the rest of the department inevitably has questions."
- **To the Builder:** "Once you have this certification, you'll have the exact tools you need to finally build that automated dashboard you've been wanting to create."

You haven't changed the task. You haven't changed the deadline. But by tailoring your language, you have connected a draining task to a fulfilling purpose.

Chapter 12: The Language of Why: Feedback, Recognition, and Motivation

Most of us were raised on the Golden Rule: *Treat others the way you want to be treated.* It is a beautiful philosophy for basic human decency, but it is a disastrous strategy for leadership.

If you are a Pioneer who loves public praise and being pulled on stage to be recognized for a wild new idea, the Golden Rule dictates that you should recognize your employees the exact same way. But what happens if your employee is a Stabilizer who is horrified by public attention and only wants a quiet, private email acknowledging their flawless execution of a difficult spreadsheet?

By applying the Golden Rule, your attempt to motivate them will actually trigger their stress response. You will have successfully alienated a top performer while trying to reward them.

To be a truly Why-Powered leader, you must abandon the Golden Rule and adopt the Platinum Rule: *Treat others the way THEY want to be treated.* You must learn to speak their language.

Every time you offer feedback, constructive criticism, or positive recognition, you are transmitting a signal. If that signal is not tuned to the receiver's specific frequency—their Why Archetype—it will be distorted into static, or worse, perceived as a threat.

The Anatomy of Meaningful Praise

We often treat praise like a generic commodity. We hand out "Great job!" or "Keep up the good work!" like cheap candy. But generic praise is forgettable. It doesn't reinforce the behaviors that actually drive high performance.

To make recognition stick, it must validate the specific source of an employee's professional dopamine.

Here is how you tailor the exact same successful project outcome into five different languages of praise:

- **Praising the Builder:** Don't just praise the effort; praise the *artifact*.
    - *Instead of:* "Great job on the website."
    - *Say:* "The architecture of this new site is incredible. You built something that is structurally sound and beautiful. I love what you created here."
- **Praising the Connector:** Don't praise them in isolation; praise their impact on the *ecosystem*.
    - *Instead of:* "You handled that client meeting well."
    - *Say:* "The way you bridged the gap between our team and the client completely shifted the energy in the

room. You brought everyone together and built a massive amount of trust."

- **Praising the Teacher:** Praise the *transfer of knowledge* and the growth of others.
    - *Instead of:* "Thanks for showing Derek how to use the software."
    - *Say:* "Derek's presentation today was flawless, and it's because of the framework you taught him. You've completely elevated his skillset."
- **Praising the Pioneer:** Praise the *courage* and the novelty of the idea.
    - *Instead of:* "Good job hitting the sales numbers."
    - *Say:* "No one else would have thought to try that unorthodox sales strategy. You pushed us out of our comfort zone, and the risk paid off brilliantly."
- **Praising the Stabilizer:** Praise the *flawless execution* and the mitigation of disaster.
    - *Instead of:* "Glad the event is over and went well."
    - *Say:* "Because you built such a rigorous contingency plan, what could have been a logistical nightmare ran perfectly smoothly. Your attention to detail saved us."

The "Yes, And" of Constructive Feedback

Delivering constructive criticism is the hardest part of a leader's job. As we learned in our dive into the neurochemistry of leadership, the moment you tell someone they did something wrong, their sympathetic nervous system is prone to hijack the conversation. Cortisol floods their system, and their brain prepares for a fight.

To bypass this defensive response, we can borrow a foundational rule from the world of improvisational theater: the principle of *"Yes, And."*

In improv comedy, if an actor steps on stage and declares, "We are stranded on a desert island!" and their scene partner replies, "No we aren't, we are in a grocery store," the scene instantly dies. The energy stops, and the actors are now in conflict. But if the partner says, *"Yes, and I think that palm tree over there has coconuts we can eat!"* the scene moves forward collaboratively.

When giving critical feedback, most leaders use "Yes, but." *"Yes, you worked hard on this, BUT the formatting is a mess."* The word "but" immediately erases the validation that came before it. It triggers the defensive reflex.

A Why-Powered leader uses "Yes, and" to align the critique with the employee's core archetype. You validate their drive, *and* you redirect their execution.

The Transparency Key: Giving Them Their "Word"

As we established earlier, the incoming workforce demands transparency. They will not blindly follow top-down directives without context. When you are redirecting an employee using the "Yes, And" framework, you must pair it with radical transparency by providing their specific "Key Word."

Every archetype needs a specific question answered before they can fully get on board with a change in direction. If you provide this specific focus, the critique stops feeling like an arbitrary punishment and starts feeling like a collaborative strategy.

- **Critiquing the Builder:** Focus on structural integrity. Give them the **WHAT**. (What is the new tangible deliverable?)
    - *"Yes, you moved incredibly fast on building this prototype, AND to make sure it doesn't break under pressure, we need to go back and reinforce the coding foundation before we ship it. **What** we need as the final deliverable is a version that can handle double the user load."*
- **Critiquing the Connector:** Focus on relational impact. Give them the **WHO**. (Who is impacted by this change?)
    - *"Yes, your passion for this project is clear, AND when you spoke over*

*Nina in the meeting, it damaged the team's trust. **Who** we need to focus on right now is the junior staff, ensuring they feel safe enough to share their ideas in the room."*

- **Critiquing the Teacher:** Focus on the clarity of the lesson. Give them the **HOW**. (How can we replicate this process?)
    - *"Yes, your depth of knowledge on this subject is unmatched, AND because you didn't document the steps, the rest of the team can impersonate your success. **How** we are going to fix this is by pausing your output for two days so you can build a step-by-step framework for the department."*
- **Critiquing the Pioneer:** Focus on the alignment of the vision. Give them the **WHY**. (Why are we changing direction?)
    - *"Yes, this new software idea is incredibly innovative, AND it doesn't align with our current Q3 budget constraints. **Why** we have to table it for now is because prioritizing the current client rollout is the only thing that will fund our R&D budget for next year."*
- **Critiquing the Stabilizer:** Focus on the flexibility of the process. Give them the **WHEN**. (When is the timeline shifting?)
    - *"Yes, your adherence to the compliance rules kept us safe, AND*

*your refusal to adapt when the client's needs changed caused a massive bottleneck. **When** timelines shift unexpectedly like this, I need you to have a flexible contingency plan ready so we don't lose momentum."*

By framing the critique through the lens of their archetype and transparently answering their core question, you aren't attacking their character; you are simply recalibrating their vehicle. You are showing them how to be a more effective version of themselves.

Building the Foundation of Trust When you consistently use your team's Key Words during difficult conversations, you are doing much more than just softening a critique. You are making a profound, long-term investment in the relationship.

By proactively providing the exact context they need—whether it's the *Why* for a Pioneer or the *Who* for a Connector—you signal that you deeply understand how their mind works. You are proving, interaction by interaction, that you truly *see* them.

This level of intentional communication builds deep, unshakeable trust. It proves that you aren't just a boss barking orders, but a leader who respects their unique operating system. In the long run, a team built on this kind of mutual understanding doesn't just survive friction; they use it to grow stronger. The relationships forged through this transparent, archetype-specific communication create a resilient, unified front that becomes the ultimate competitive advantage for your entire organization.

The Currency of Motivation

Feedback and recognition are not just HR requirements; they are the currency you use to purchase your team's discretionary effort. If you pay a Pioneer in the currency of a Stabilizer, the transaction will fail.

When you learn to speak the Language of Why fluently, your feedback stops being a source of anxiety and starts becoming a powerful tool for alignment.

But what happens when you aren't the only one in the room? What happens when a Pioneer and a Stabilizer are forced to collaborate on a high-stakes project, and their differing languages cause them to completely, fundamentally clash?

In the next chapter, we will look at the final piece of the puzzle: how to manage the friction and build a truly Why-Powered Team Culture.

Chapter 13: Building a Why-Powered Team Culture: Managing the Friction

Up until this point, we have focused heavily on the individual. You have learned how to discover your own leadership drive, how to uncover your employees' archetypes, and how to tailor their roles and feedback to match their native language.

But leadership rarely happens in a vacuum. You are not just managing individuals; you are managing an ecosystem. And in any ecosystem, when different elements collide, you get friction.

In traditional management, friction is viewed as a failure. If two employees are arguing over a project, the traditional boss steps in, tells them to "be professional," and forces a compromise where neither person is happy.

A Why-Powered leader views friction entirely differently. In physics, friction is simply resistance that generates heat and energy. Unmanaged, it causes fires and burns the team out. But managed correctly, friction is the exact mechanism that gives a tire traction on the road. It is the force that propels the vehicle forward.

When you have a team made up of diverse archetypes, conflict is not a sign of dysfunction; it is a sign that your people care deeply about their work. The conflict arises because their sources of fulfillment—their *Whys*—are fundamentally opposed. Your job is not to eliminate the friction. Your job is to act as the bilingual translator who helps them understand each other.

The Friction Pairings

Certain archetypes, by their very nature, are designed to pull in opposite directions. Here are the most common "Friction Pairings" you will encounter, why they clash, and the exact translation scripts you can use to mediate the conflict and generate forward momentum.

Friction Pairing #1: The Pioneer vs. The Stabilizer

The Core Conflict: Innovation vs. Risk Mitigation. The Pioneer wants to break the system to find a better way. The Stabilizer wants to reinforce the system to prevent a disaster. To the Pioneer, the Stabilizer is a bureaucratic wet blanket. To the Stabilizer, the Pioneer is a reckless liability.

The Scenario: Ethan (Pioneer) wants to immediately switch the team to a brand new, untested project management software because it has exciting AI features. Zoe (Stabilizer) is blocking the purchase, demanding a three-month security review and data-migration contingency plan. They are currently arguing in your office.

The Translation Script: As the leader, you must step in and translate their motives using their Key

Words (*Why* for the Pioneer, *When* for the Stabilizer).

- **To Ethan (Pioneer):** "Ethan, I love the **Why** behind this. You are trying to innovate and save us time, which is exactly what I need you to do. But **When** you try to implement it overnight, you trigger Zoe's job, which is to protect our data. She isn't trying to kill your idea; she's trying to make sure your idea doesn't crash the company."
- **To Zoe (Stabilizer):** "Zoe, I deeply value how you protect us. But **When** you demand a three-month review for a pilot program, you are suffocating the innovation we need to stay competitive. Ethan isn't trying to be reckless; he's trying to future-proof us."
- **The Resolution:** "Here is the traction: Ethan, you get a sandbox. You can migrate five non-essential projects to the new software this week to test it. Zoe, you are in charge of defining the exact security metrics Ethan's pilot program has to hit before we ever consider a department-wide rollout."

Friction Pairing #2: The Builder vs. The Connector

The Core Conflict: Task Execution vs. Social Harmony. The Builder wants to put their head down, ignore the politics, and just get the product finished. The Connector wants to ensure that every stakeholder feels heard and that the team is happy during the process. To the Builder, the Connector is wasting time talking. To the Connector, the Builder is cold, abrasive, and damaging relationships.

The Scenario: Liam (Builder) has locked himself in a conference room to finish the code for a new website. Ava (Connector) keeps interrupting him, insisting they need to hold a sync meeting with the marketing team to ensure everyone feels good about the design direction. Liam snaps at her, and now Ava is upset.

The Translation Script: Translate using their Key Words (*What* for the Builder, *Who* for the Connector).

- **To Liam (Builder):** "Liam, your dedication to the **What**—the actual product—is incredible. But right now, you are building in a silo. If you alienate Ava and the marketing team, it doesn't matter how flawless your code is; they won't support the launch. Ava is trying to protect the adoption of the very thing you are building."
- **To Ava (Connector):** "Ava, your focus on **Who** is impacted by this project is the glue of this team. But Liam gets his energy from deep, uninterrupted creation. Every time you pull him into a sync meeting, you break his flow state. He isn't ignoring the team; he is trying to deliver for them."
- **The Resolution:** "Here is the traction: Liam, I need you to give Ava a 15-minute briefing

every morning at 9:00 a.m. on your exact progress. Ava, you are the shield. You take that information, handle the marketing team, and protect Liam's calendar from any interruptions for the rest of the day."

Friction Pairing #3: The Teacher vs. The Builder

The Core Conflict: The Process vs. The Product. The Teacher wants to explain the theory behind the work and ensure everyone understands *how* to do it. The Builder just wants to get the work done and move on to the next tangible deliverable. To the Teacher, the Builder is impatient and careless. To the Builder, the Teacher is pedantic and lecturing.

The Scenario: A Teacher is trying to explain the entire history of a coding language to a Builder who just wants the specific line of code needed to fix a bug. The Builder rolls their eyes, and the Teacher feels deeply disrespected.

The Translation Script: Translate using their Key Words (*How* for the Teacher, *What* for the Builder).

- **To the Builder:** "Your focus on exactly **What** needs to be fixed right now is why you are so efficient. But when you dismiss the explanation, you are shutting down the Teacher's core drive. They aren't trying to lecture you; they are trying to empower you so you don't need to ask for help next time."

- **To the Teacher:** "Your dedication to **How** this works is why you are our expert. But the Builder's brain is currently locked onto the immediate deliverable. If you give them a 20-minute theory lesson when they are trying to put out a fire, they can't hear you."
- **The Resolution:** "Here is the traction: Builder, let the Teacher give you the quick context before you take the tool. Teacher, give the Builder the exact fix they need immediately, and then schedule a 10-minute follow-up later to document the theory when the fire is out."

The Ultimate Goal: A Self-Translating Team

As a leader, you start by being the translator. But your ultimate goal is to make your job obsolete.

You build a true, Why-Powered team culture when you teach the framework to your employees. When the team understands the Five Archetypes, they stop taking friction personally.

When Ethan (Pioneer) understands that Zoe is a Stabilizer, he stops thinking she is a control freak who hates his ideas. He realizes that her default way of looking at the world is to mitigate risk—whether that is how she is naturally wired or how years of experience have conditioned her to operate. With that understanding, he learns to approach her differently: *"Zoe, I have a wild idea, but before I pitch it, can you help me spot the security risks?"*

When that happens, the magic unlocks. The Pioneer and the Stabilizer stop fighting each other and start fighting the problem together.

Embedding the Language: Culture Rituals

To make this stick, the Language of Why must become part of your daily operational cadence. It requires radical transparency. Here are two rituals to embed this in your culture:

1. The "Why" Kickoff At the start of any major new project, don't just assign tasks. Go around the room and explicitly state the "Why" alignment for each person. *"Liam, you are our Builder; you own the prototype. Ava, you are our Connector; you own the client communication. Zoe, as our Stabilizer, you own the timeline and risk assessment."* This publicly validates their strengths and sets clear boundaries for collaboration.

2. Purpose-Driven Shoutouts At the end of your weekly team meetings, dedicate five minutes to peer-to-peer recognition, but require the team to use the Language of Why. Don't let them just say, "Thanks to Ethan for his hard work." Encourage them to say, "I want to shout out Ethan for being a true Pioneer this week and finding a completely new way to bypass that software glitch."

When your team starts recognizing the intrinsic motives of their peers, you have successfully moved from managing a group of individuals to leading a connected, high-performing culture.

You have built the foundation. You have learned the language. You have managed the friction. There is only one question left: How do we measure the results?

In Part 5, we will look at the true ROI of a purpose-driven team.

Part 5: The Ripple Effect

Chapter 14: Measuring What Matters: The ROI of a Purpose-Driven Team

If you implement the tools in this book—if you shift your feedback to match the Language of Why, if you carve out 20% of your team's week for aligned work, and if you manage friction through the lens of the Five Archetypes—you will feel the change in your team almost immediately. Meetings will be more energetic, conflicts will resolve faster, and the general mood of the department will lift.

But "good vibes" do not satisfy a board of directors, and they don't secure your budget for next year.

To make purpose-driven leadership a permanent fixture in your organization, you must be able to prove its Return on Investment. You have to translate human fulfillment into business metrics.

Lagging vs. Leading Indicators

Most companies measure employee engagement through lagging indicators. They look at annual turnover rates, exit interviews, and yearly performance reviews. The problem with a lagging indicator is that by the time you see the data, the damage is already done. The veteran employee with all the institutional knowledge has already left. The toxic conflict has already derailed the project.

A Why-Powered leader tracks leading indicators. These are the real-time metrics that prove your team is operating in a state of high psychological safety and deep alignment.

1. The Velocity of Trust (Speed to Execution)

When a Pioneer and a Stabilizer are misaligned, a project might sit in committee for six weeks while they argue. When they understand each other's "Why," that same project moves from ideation to execution in six days. You measure this by tracking the time it takes to move a project from the kickoff meeting to the first tangible milestone. When your team is aligned, the friction drops, and the velocity of execution skyrockets.

2. The Shift in Innovation (Discretionary Effort)

Are your employees only doing exactly what is on their job description, or are they actively looking for ways to improve the system? When a Builder feels seen, they don't just finish the assigned report; they build a macro that automates the report for the whole department. Track the number of unsolicited, proactive ideas or improvements generated by your team. This discretionary effort is the purest metric of intrinsic motivation.

3. The Employee Net Promoter Score (eNPS)

While traditional engagement surveys are often too long and infrequent, a simple, quarterly eNPS asks one question: *"On a scale of 1-10, how likely are you to recommend working on this team to a friend?"* A high eNPS directly correlates to a team that feels seen, valued, and aligned with their core drivers.

The Implementation Gap: Why Reading Isn't Enough

Understanding these metrics and the Five Archetypes gives you a massive advantage. But knowing the framework and successfully embedding it into the DNA of your company are two entirely different things.

This brings us to a harsh reality: handing a book to your management team will not magically fix your company culture.

Time and time again, I see well-intentioned executives read about purpose-driven leadership, get excited, and declare a "culture shift" on Monday morning. By Friday, everyone is back to their old habits. They fall into the Implementation Gap.

If you are trying to roll this out across an organization or even a large department, you must actively guard against these three fatal pitfalls:

Pitfall 1: The "One and Done" Exercise
Leadership introduces the Why Archetypes at an annual off-site retreat. Everyone takes the assessment, laughs about their results, and maybe puts their archetype in their email signature. Then, the retreat ends. The framework is never integrated into 1-on-1s, performance reviews, or project kickoff meetings. The archetypes become a forgotten novelty rather than a daily operating system.

Pitfall 2: Misaligned Corporate Systems You cannot manage a team using the Language of Why if your HR department is still enforcing a rigid, industrial-era performance review system. If you tell a Connector that you value their ability to unify the team, but their official yearly bonus is tied strictly to cutthroat, individual sales metrics, the system will crush your leadership efforts. The structural incentives must align with the cultural message.

Pitfall 3: The Facilitation Wall This is the most common roadblock. A leader understands the concepts perfectly, but they lack the objective distance required to facilitate these deep conversations with their own team. When a boss tries to uncover a team's dysfunctions, employees often withhold the truth out of fear. The psychological safety simply isn't there yet. Furthermore, managing the complex dynamics of a room full of mixed archetypes requires a very specific facilitation skillset that most operational leaders haven't been trained in.

Bridging the Gap

When a company hits the Facilitation Wall, the friction usually intensifies. The team learns the vocabulary of the archetypes, but without an objective guide, they weaponize the terms. ("I didn't finish the report because I'm a Pioneer, I don't do details!")

This is exactly why systemic culture change almost always requires an outside perspective. An external facilitator does not have a stake in the company politics. They bring the objective authority necessary to cut through the defensive postures, establish immediate psychological safety, and guide the team through the growing pains of adopting a new language.

They can conduct the Life & Leadership Audits for the executive team, ensuring the leaders are fully aligned before they try to lead others. They can host the interactive workshops that move the archetypes from a theory on a page to a living, breathing conflict-resolution tool.

You have the map in your hands. But if you want to move your entire organization across the bridge without losing momentum, you don't have to do it alone.

Chapter 15: The End of Management, The Beginning of Leadership

In the introduction of this book, I told you about my dream job. I told you about the cross-country move, the cat in the carrier under the seat, and the adrenaline of finally making it.

I also told you about the heartbreak that followed. I told you what it felt like to be managed by a boss who only saw a job description, not a human being. I remember the distinct feeling of being a ghost in the hallways of my own career, completely invisible to the people who were supposed to be guiding me.

That experience left a scar, but it also left a mandate. It forced me to ask a question that ultimately changed the trajectory of my life: *What would have happened if my leader had actually seen me?* What if, instead of telling me to stop being friends with my coworkers, they had recognized my Connector drive and empowered me to build cross-departmental bridges? What if they had tapped into my Teacher archetype and allowed me to design the wellness programs we had talked about in my interview?

I wouldn't have just stayed at that company; I would have fought for it. I would have given them my absolute highest level of discretionary effort. I would have been a force multiplier for their mission.

Instead, I became a statistic.

Every single day, in office buildings and on job sites around the world, brilliant, capable people are quietly checking out. They are taking their institutional knowledge, their creativity, and their potential, and they are walking out the door—not because the work is too hard, but because the environment is too disconnected.

Management is the act of organizing resources to hit a target. You manage a budget. You manage a timeline. You manage a supply chain.

But you cannot manage a human heart. You cannot mandate inspiration, and you cannot put a metric on trust.

Leadership is the act of connecting an individual's internal drive to a shared external outcome. It is the hard, necessary, and deeply rewarding work of being an archeologist of human potential.

When you shift from being a manager of tasks to a leader of people, everything changes.

- You stop talking at your team and start listening to understand.
- You stop trying to motivate everyone with the same generic corporate mission statement and start speaking the specific Language of Why.

- You stop seeing team friction as a nuisance and start using it as traction.

You become the Head Coach who runs alongside them in the marathon.

The industrial-era playbook is dead. The incoming workforce will not tolerate being treated as a replaceable cog, and the outgoing workforce is taking their wisdom with them. The only leaders who will survive and thrive in this new landscape are the ones who understand that empathy is not a soft skill; it is an economic imperative.

You now have the framework. You know the five archetypes—the Builder, the Connector, the Teacher, the Pioneer, and the Stabilizer. You know how to tailor their roles, how to give them feedback that actually resonates, and how to turn their differences into your greatest competitive advantage.

The revolving door of talent does not have to be your reality. You have the power to stop the cycle.

It is time to put down the spreadsheets and look at the human beings standing right in front of you. It's time to be the leader they are waiting for.

Don't just be visible. Be seen. And then, go see them.

Your Journey Continues: Keep Going with HiVis Hoodie

Reading this book is a powerful first step, but the real transformation happens when you move from theory into consistent practice. You do not have to cross the Implementation Gap alone.

Whether you are an individual leader looking to optimize your own career, or an executive looking to overhaul an entire corporate culture, here is how we can continue the work together:

1. Take the Official "Why Type" Assessment

Stop guessing and start knowing. While this book provides the clues, the official assessment provides the definitive data. Discover your dominant and secondary archetypes, and receive a customized motivational profile detailing exactly how you operate at your highest level.

- **Get your profile:** meaganhopper.com/assessment

2. Claim Your Free "Why-Powered Leader" Toolkit

To help you put the concepts from this book into immediate practice on Monday morning, I have created a free digital toolkit for your desk. It includes the "Archeologist's Question Bank" to revitalize your 1-on-1 meetings, the "Open Table" agenda template for your next project kickoff, and the "Language of Why" quick-reference cheat sheet so you always know exactly how to tailor your feedback to the five archetypes.

- **Download it here:** meaganhopper.com/workbook

3. Customized Full-Picture Coaching

You cannot be a burned-out human at 5:59 p.m. and a purpose-driven leader at 9:00 a.m. My 1-on-1 coaching is highly tailored to your unique needs, starting with a comprehensive Life & Leadership Audit. Delivered over a focused 4-month term with an accessible per-month structure, we look closely at all aspects of your life—not just your 9-to-5—to ensure you aren't just performing well as a leader, but truly allowing yourself to thrive as a whole human being. Because this work is so deep and individualized, I am very selective and only work with a few private clients at a time.

- **Explore coaching:** meaganhopper.com/coaching

4. Corporate Workshops & Team Facilitation

Handing this book to your team is a great start, but changing a company culture requires objective, expert facilitation. Bring me in to guide your team through the growing pains of adopting a new language. Through interactive workshops, we will move the Five Archetypes from a theory on a page into a daily, conflict-resolving operating system for your entire organization.

- **Book a team training:** meaganhopper.com/corporate

5. Keynote Speaking

Looking to inspire your organization at your next conference or all-hands meeting? I deliver high-energy, actionable keynotes on authentic communication, navigating generational shifts in the workplace, and the bottom-linc ROI of empathetic leadership.

- **Watch my TEDx talk and book me to speak:** meaganhopper.com/speaking

Let's stay connected. Join the community of leaders who are changing the way we work.

- **Website:** meaganhopper.com
- **LinkedIn:** linkedin.com/company/hivishoodie
- **Instagram:** @hivishoodie